MW00781404

Keda Mazbuut

Keda Mazbuut

A Grammar Book of
EGYPTIAN ARABIC
with Exercises

Mona Kamel Hassan

The American University in Cairo Press
Cairo   New York

First published in 2020 by
The American University in Cairo Press
113 Sharia Kasr el Aini, Cairo, Egypt
One Rockefeller Plaza, 10th Floor, New York, NY 10020
www.aucpress.com

Dar el Kutub No. 23527/18
ISBN 978 977 416 923 6

Dar el Kutub Cataloging-in-Publication Data

Hassan, Mona Kamel
        Keda Mazbuut: A Grammar Book of Egyptian Colloquial Arabic with Exercises /
    Mona Kamel Hassan.—Cairo: The American University in Cairo Press, 2020.
        p.   cm.
        ISBN 978 977 416 923 6
        1. English Language—Grammar study and teaching—foreign speakers
        425

1 2 3 4 5   24 23 22 21 20

Designed by Rafik Abousoliman
Printed in the United States of America

Contents

Preface

This book is a compilation of grammatical structures of Egyptian Colloquial Arabic (ECA) and adopts a communicative approach. It targets learners of Arabic as a foreign language (AFL) at an elementary language-proficiency level. It contains twenty-five lessons which gradually introduce grammatical rules, from the simplest to the more difficult. Explanation of these grammatical rules is provided in English whereas the examples accompanying the explanation are provided in Arabic and in transliteration. Each lesson includes various exercises encouraging AFL learners to competently communicate with native speakers using ECA in different uncomplicated situations. In addition, supplementary MP3 files of the audio material, which aim to facilitate the pronunciation of the Arabic content included in the book, are available on the American University of Cairo Press's SoundCloud account. AFL learners are encouraged to go through the explanation provided for each lesson independently. Thus, instead of taking a lot of the class time to explain the grammatical rules, teachers will devote this time to answering students' questions and working on the exercises of each lesson, which require a lot of speaking.

This grammar reference book will help AFL learners and AFL teachers, as well as scholars and linguists interested in the grammar of the Egyptian dialect.

To access the supplementary audio material for this book, visit www. aucpress.com/arabic or scan this QR code:

Acknowledgments

My gratitude goes first to my students at the Center for Arabic Study Abroad (CASA) and my Arabic Language Instruction (ALI) colleague Dr. Shahira Yacout, who inspired me to write this book. Many thanks also go to Ms. Rasha Essam, head of the ALI Computer-Assisted Language Learning (CALL) Unit at the American University in Cairo (AUC), for all the great efforts she exerted in developing the supplementary MP3 files of the audio material. My ALI colleague Ms. Hala Yehia deserves my appreciation for agreeing to record the Arabic content of the book. I also thank my ALI colleague Dr. Dalal Abo El Seoud for going through the book and giving me her fruitful comments as well as the book reviewers who provided me with their constructive feedback. Last but not least, I thank both Mr. Tarek Ghanem from the AUC Press for his great advice, support, and cooperation and Ms. Ælfwine Mischler for her great help in editing and formatting the manuscript.

Egyptian Colloquial Arabic Phonetic Symbols

This list of the phonetic symbols is adapted from the International Phonetic Alphabet (IPA), with a few necessary modifications.

Consonants

ʔ	ء	voiceless glottal plosive
b	ب	voiced bilabial plosive
t	ت	voiceless alveolar plosive
g	ج	voiced velar plosive
ħ	ح	voiceless pharyngeal fricative
x	خ	voiceless uvular fricative
d	د	voiced alveolar plosive
ð	ذ	voiced dental plosive (is switched to either a ز "z" or a د "d" in ECA)
r	ر	voiced alveolar trill
z	ز	voiced alveolar fricative
s	س	voiceless alveolar fricative
ʃ	ش	voiceless palato-alveolar fricative
ş	ص	voiceless pharyngealized (emphatic) alveolar fricative
ḑ	ض	voiced pharyngealized (emphatic) alveolar plosive
ţ	ط	voiceless pharyngealized (emphatic) alveolar plosive
z̧	ظ	voiced pharyngealized (emphatic) alveolar fricative
ʒ	ع	voiced pharyngeal fricative
ɣ	غ	voiced uvular fricative
f	ف	voiceless labiodental fricative

q   ق   voiceless uvular plosive

In Egyptian Colloquial Arabic, the ق (q) is often pronounced as ء (ʔ), the voiceless glottal plosive, however, in some words the pronunciation of ق does not change. These exceptions should be memorized.

k   ك   voiceless velar plosive
l   ل   voiced dental lateral
m   م   voiced bilabial nasal
n   ن   voiced dental nasal
h   ه   voiceless glottal fricative

Semi-Vowels

w   و   voiced bilabial glide
y   ي   voiced palatal glide

Vowels

a   high-low front unrounded vowel
ɑ   a vowel that always occurs with emphatic consonants and sometimes with other consonants (with the pronunciation the same in both cases), as in the English word 'bar'
i   high front unrounded vowel
u   high back rounded vowel
e   as in the English word *bent*
ee   high-mid front unrounded vowel like the 'ai' in the English words 'straight' and 'fail'
o   high-mid back rounded vowel as in the English word 'boat'

These vowels occur in both short and long forms.
Long vowels are indicated by doubling the vowel.
Gemminated consonants are indicated by doubling the consonant letter.
A hyphen (-) marks elisions at word junctions.

Abbreviations

The following abbreviations are used throughout the book:
- m. masculine
- f. feminine
- s. singular
- d. dual
- p. plural

Lesson 1: Singular Nouns

Singular Feminine Nouns

Most singular feminine nouns (المفرد المؤنث) end with a ة/ـة *(ta marbuutʿa)* in their written forms.

مَكْتَبَة	maktaba	library

Singular Masculine Nouns

Singular masculine nouns (المفرد المذكر) do not end with a ة/ـة *(ta marbuutʿa)*.

مَكْتَب	maktab	desk, office

Exceptions

However, there are some singular feminine nouns that do not end with a ة/ـة *(ta marbuutʿa)*. These nouns should be memorized.

بِنْت	bint	girl
شَمْس	ʃams	sun

Exercise 1
Choose the masculine nouns from the words below and pronounce each of them.

بِيت	جَامْعَة	مُدِيرَة	جَزْمَة
home, house	university	director	shoes
قِسْم	أَرْض	خِير	قَلَم
department	floor, ground	good	pen
نادي	دَرْس	طَالِب	شَقَّة
club	lesson	student	apartment
نَضَّارَة	شَارِع	سُوق	أُوضَة
glasses	street	market	room

أُسْتَاذَة	مَطْعَم	كُمْبِيُوتَر	سَاعَة
teacher, professor (f.)	restaurant	computer	clock, watch, hour
قَمِيص	بَنْك	مَكْتَب	دُكْتُور
shirt	bank	desk, office	doctor (physician or PhD holder)
مُهَنْدِسَة	أُتُوبِيس	كُرْسِي	كِتَاب
engineer	bus	chair	book
جُرْنَال	صُورَة	تِلِيفِزْيُون	رَاديُو
journal, newspaper	picture, photograph	television	radio
دُور	حَمَّام	تَرابِيزَة	مُوَظَّف
floor, turn, role	bathroom	table	employee
صَاحْبَة	شَاي	قَهْوَة	مَيَّة
friend	tea	coffee	water
قَامُوس	عِنْوان	حِسَاب	واجِب
dictionary	address, title	bill	homework
شُغْل	هَرَم	ظَرْف	صَبَاح
work	pyramid	envelope, circumstance	morning
ضُهْر	زَعْلان	يَمِين	غَرْب
noon	upset	right	west

Exercise 2
Choose the feminine nouns from the table in exercise 1 and pronounce each of them.

Lesson 2: The Definite Article

The Definite Article: الـ التعريف

To change an indefinite Arabic noun or adjective into a definite one, a prefix الـ (transliteration: *il*; meaning: the) is attached to the noun or adjective.

باب baab (a door) becomes الباب ilbaab (the door).
واسع waasiȝ (wide) becomes الواسع ilwaasiȝ (the wide).

Sun and Moon Letters

When the definite article is attached to Arabic nouns and adjectives, one has to consider sun letters (الحروف الشمسية) and moon letters (الحروف القمرية) in the pronunciation.

Sun Letters	Transcribed Form	Moon Letters	Transcribed Form
ت	t	ء	ʔ
ث*	Pronounced either as s (ت) or as t (س)	ب	b
ج	g	ح	ħ
د	d	خ	x
ذ*	Pronounced either as z (ز) or as d (د)	ع	ȝ
ر	r	غ	ɣ
ز	z	ف	f
س	s	ق*	Pronounced either as q or as ʔ (ء)
ش	ʃ	م	m
ص	ş	هـ	h
ض	ԁ̣	و	w
ط	ţ	ي	y
ظ	z̧		
ك	k		

ل	l		
ن	n		

☽ Nouns and adjectives starting with a moon letter

When the prefix الـ (*il*) is attached to Arabic nouns and adjectives starting with a moon letter, it is written and pronounced as الـ (*il*).

Written Form	Pronunciation
باب → الْباب	baab → ilbaab (door → the door)

☽ Nouns and adjectives starting with a sun letter

However, when the prefix الـ (*il*) is attached to Arabic nouns and adjectives starting with a sun letter, it is written الـ (*il*) but when it is pronounced, the ل (*l*) sound is dropped and the sun letter at the beginning of the word is doubled.

Written Form	Pronunciation
شَمْس → الشَّمْس	ʃams → iʃʃams (sun → the sun)
كِتاب → الْكِّتاب	ketaab → ikketaab (book → the book)

Exercise 1

Choose the words with sun letters from the following table, then add the definite article الـ (*il*) to each word and pronounce it.

بِيت	جامْعَة	مُديرَة	جَزْمَة
home, house	university	director	shoes
قِسْم	أَرْض	خِير	قَلَم
department	floor, Earth, ground	good	pen

شَقَّة	طالِب	دَرْس	نادي
apartment	student	lesson	club
أُوضَة	سُوق	شارِع	نَضّارَة
room	market	street	glasses
أُسْتاذَة	مَطْعَم	كُمْبِيُوتَر	ساعَة
teacher, professor (f.)	restaurant	computer	clock, watch, hour
قَمِيص	بَنْك	مَكْتَب	دُكْتُور
shirt	bank	desk, office	doctor (physician or PhD holder)
مُهَنْدِسَة	أُتُوبِيس	كُرْسِي	كِتاب
engineer	bus	chair	book
جُرْنال	صُورَة	تِلِيفِزْيُون	راذْيُو
journal, newspaper	picture, photograph	television	radio
دُور	حَمّام	تَرابِيزَة	مُوَظَّف
floor, turn, role	bathroom	table	employee
صاحْبَة	شاي	قَهْوَة	مَيَّة
friend	tea	coffee	water
قامُوس	عِنْوان	حِساب	واجِب
dictionary	address, title	bill	homework
شُغْل	هَرَم	ظَرْف	صَباح
work	pyramid	envelope, circumstance	morning
ضُهْر	زَعْلان	يِمِين	غَرْب
noon	upset	right	west

Exercise 2

Choose the words with moon letters from the table in exercise 1, then add the definite article الـ (*il*) to each word and pronounce it.

Lesson 3: Demonstrative Pronouns

There are three demonstrative pronouns (أسماء الإشارة) that can be used either before or after nouns:

This/that for singular masculine
دَه/دا da/dah
This/that for singular feminine and for non-human plural
دي di
These/those for masculine and feminine dual, and for human plural
دول dool

When a demonstrative pronoun occurs before an indefinite noun, a complete sentence is formed.

دا كِتـاب.	da ketaab	This is a book.

If a demonstrative pronoun occurs after a definite noun, it forms a phrase that does not make a complete sentence on its own.

الـكـتـاب دا	ikketaab da	This book is

Exercise 1
Choose the correct demonstrative pronoun for each sentence.

Example:

_____ كُمْبِيُوتَر.
(دا / دِي / دُول)

الطَّالِبَة _____ مِــن أمـرِيــكــا.
(دا / دِي / دُول)

٦- _____ أُوضَة.
(دا / دِي / دُول)

١- _____ شارِع.
(دا / دِي / دُول)

٧- الشَّقَّة في البيت _____ .
(دا / دِي / دُول)

٢- _____ قَلَم ووَرَقَة.
(دا / دِي / دُول)

٨- هي في المـدْرَسَة _____ .
(دا / دِي / دُول)

٣- _____ العِنْوان.
(دا / دِي / دُول)

٩- إحْنـا في الفَصْل _____ .
(دا / دِي / دُول)

٤- _____ مُدرّسة.
(دا / دِي / دُول)

١٠- السّت والرّاجِل _____ مِن أمْرِيـكا.
(دا / دِي / دُول)

٥- الكِتاب _____ كِتاب الأُسْتـاذ.
(دا / دِي / دُول)

Exercise 2
Make a video with your mobile phone or camera showing ten items in your room, apartment, or university using the demonstrative pronouns (دا / دِي / دُول) and send it to your teacher.

Lesson 4: The Verb 'to Be'

Absence of the Present Tense of the Verb 'to Be'

In an Arabic nominal sentence (الجملة الاسمية) in the present tense, the verb 'to be' is only implied in the personal pronouns used. In other cases, the verb 'to be' is neither written nor pronounced.

هِيَّ هِنا.	heyya hena	She is here.

Here هِيَّ (heyya) (she) carries the meaning of "she is."

Personal Pronouns

There are eight personal pronouns (الضمائر) in Egyptian Colloquial Arabic:

Singular			Dual and Plural		
هُوّ	huwwa	he	هُمَّ	humma	they (m. / f.)
هِيَّ	heyya	she			
إنتَ	?enta	you (m.)	إنْتُو	?entu	you (m. / f.)
إنْتي	?enti	you (f.)			
أنا	?ana	I	إحْنا	?eħna	we

Negation (مِش)

The word مِش (transliteration: *miʃ*; meaning: not) is inserted after the personal pronoun to apply negation. Note that the verb 'to be' is still only implied in the present tense in cases of negation.

هِيَّ مِش هِنا.	heyya miʃ hena	She is not here.

There is/There are (فيه)

فيه *(fiih)* is used to express existence.

فِيه كِتاب عَلَى المَكْتَب.	fiih ketaab ʒala-ilmaktab
There is a book on the desk.	
فِيه طَلَبَة في الفصل؟	fiih ʈalaba f-ilfaṣl
Are there students in the classroom?	

Negation of Existence

Insert the prefix مَ (ma) and the suffix ش (ʃ) so that فِيــه (fiih) becomes مَفِيش (mafiiʃ) to negate something's existence.

مَفِيش كِتـاب عَلَى الـمَكْتَب.	mafiiʃ ketaab ʒala-ilmaktab
There is no book on the desk.	
مَفِيش طَلَبَة في الفصـل.	mafiiʃ ʈalaba f-ilfaṣl
There are no students in the classroom.	

Exercise 1
Choose the correct translation for each sentence.

Example:
There is no movie now.

- دا مِش فيـلْم دِلْـوَقْـتـي.
- فيـه فيـلْم دِلْـوَقْـتـي.
- مَفيش فيـلْم دِلْـوَقْـتـي

1. This is an apartment.

- فيـه شـقَّـة.
- دِي شـقَّـة.
- مَفِيش شـقَّـة.

2. There is no lesson.

- دا مِش درس.
- فيـه درس.
- مـفيـش درس.

3. These are the watch and the glasses.

- فيـه سـاعـة ونضـارة
- دول الـسـاعـة والنضـارة
- الـسـاعـة والنضـارة دول

4. There is milk.

- دا لَبَن.
- مِفِيش لَبَن.
- فيه لَبَن.

5. The director is here.

- فيه مدير هِنا.
- المدِير هِنا.
- المدير مش هنا.

6. There is no market.

- دا مِش سُوق.
- فيه سُوق.
- مفيش سُوق.

7. The girl is in the classroom.

- البنت فِي الفَصْل.
- فيه بنت فِي الفَصْل.
- مفيش بنت فِي الفَصْل.

8. The house is on this street.

- دا بيت فِي الشارِع.
- البيت فِي الشارِع دا.
- فيه بيت فِي الشارِع دا.

9. I am in this bank.

- أنا فِي البنك.
- أنا مِش فِي البنك.
- أنا فِي البنك دا.

10. She is not here.

- هِيَّ هِنا.
- دِي مِش هِنا.
- هِيَّ مِش هِنا.

Exercise 2
Make a video with your mobile phone or camera stating which items in the table below are in your apartment and which items are not. Send the video to your teacher.

صالُون	سَتـايِر	سِجَّادَة	سُفْرة
قَزايِز	تـابْلُوهات	كَراسِي	تِرابِيزَة
كُتُب	كُمبِيُوتَر	مَكْتَبَة	نَجَف
تِلِيفِزْيُون	راذْيُو	سِرير	طَبَق

Lesson 5: Interrogatives

Egyptian Colloquial Arabic interrogatives (أدوات الاستفهام) can occur at the beginning, in the middle, or at the end of a sentence. The following is a table of the interrogatives used in Egyptian Colloquial Arabic, with examples.

Interrogative	Transliterated Form	Examples and English Translation
فـيـن where	feen	الـجامْعَة فِين؟ iggamʒa feen? Where is the university?
مـيـن who	miin	مـيـن الـمُدَرّس؟ miin ilmudarris? Who is the teacher?
لـيـه why	leeh	هُوَّ زَعْلان لِيه؟ huwwa zaʒlaan leeh Why is he upset?
إيـه what	ʔeeh	إيـه دا؟ ʔeeh da What is this?
إمْـتَـى when	ʔemta	الـدَّرْس إمْـتَـى؟ ʔeddars ʔemta When is the class?
من إمـتـى since when	min ʔemta	هُوَّ فِـي مَصْـر مِن إمْـتَـى؟ huwwa f-maṣr min ʔemta? How long has he been in Egypt?
مِنِين from where	mineen	هِـيَّ مِنِين؟ heyya mineen? Where is she from?
كـام + singular noun how many	kaam	عـايِز كـام كِتـاب؟ ʒaayiz kaam ketaab? How many books do you want?
بِكـام how much	bikaam	الـبُرْتُـقـان بِكـام؟ ilburtuʔaan bikaam? How much are the oranges?

قَدَ إيـه how much, how long	?addi-?eeh	عايِز سُكَّر قَدَ إيه؟ ȝaayiz sukkarr ?addi-?eeh? How much sugar do you want? قَعَد في مَصْر قَدَ إيه؟ ?aȝad fi-maṣr ?addi-?eeh? How long did he stay in Egypt?
أَنْـهُو (m.) أَنْـهِي (f.) which	?anhu ?anhi	ساكِن في أنهو دُور؟ saakin fi ?anhu door? Which floor do you live on? ساكِن في أنهي شَقَّة؟ saakin fi ?anhi ʃa??a? Which apartment do you live in?
إزّاي how	?ezzaay	عايِز الشّاي إزّاي؟ ȝaayiz iʃʃaay ?ezzaay? How do you want the tea?

Exercise 1
Choose the correct interrogative for each sentence.

Example:

إنْـتَ _____ دِلْوَقْتِـي؟
(لِيـه – فِيـن – بـكـام)

١- يوسِف هِنـا _____ ؟
(مِين – لِيـه – بـكـام)

٢- الـكـتـاب والـقـلـم _____ ؟
(فِين – مِين – إمتَى)

٣- _____ دا؟
(إمتَى – لِيـه – إيـه)

٤- الأجازة _____ ؟
(مِين – إمْتَى – بـكـام)

٥ـ بِيت لَيْلَى _____ ؟
(فِين – لِيـه – مِـيـن)

٦ـ القَمِيص _____ ؟
(إمـتَـى – بـكـام – كـام)

٧ـ هِـيَّ _____ ؟
(كـام – لِيـه – مِنين)

٨ـ عـايِز _____ قَلَم؟
(مِـين – كـام – فِين)

٩ـ الفِطـار _____ ؟
(لِيـه – مِين – فِين)

١٠ـ الحفْلـة _____ ؟
(مِـين – إمْـتَـى – كـام)

Exercise 2
Form questions for which the sentences given are the answers.

Example:

الفِيلْم إمْتَـى؟
الفِيلْم دِلْوَقْتِي.

_____ ١ـ
دِي لَيْلَى.

_____ ٢ـ
هُمَّ مِن إيطـالْيـا.

_____ ٣ـ
دا قَلَم.

_____ ٤ـ
الـدَرْس دِلْوَقْتِي.

‏٥_
‏_____

‏لأ. هُوَّ مِش مُهَنْدِس.

‏٦_
‏_____

‏الْمُوز بِـ ١٠ جِنِيه.

‏٧_
‏_____

‏دُول ٥ كُتُب.

‏٨_
‏_____

‏يُوسِف فِي الْمَطْعَم.

‏٩_
‏_____

‏لَيْلَى ساكْنة فِي خامِس دُور.

‏١٠_
‏_____

‏يُوسِف فِي الْجَامْعَة عَشــان مَفِيش أجازَة النَّهارْدَه.

Lesson 6: *Nisba* Adjectives

Definition of *Nisba* (نسبة) Adjectives

Nisba adjectives indicate relationships and they are formed by adding a suffix to a noun. Adding the suffix ي *(i)* to a noun forms a singular masculine adjective, the suffix يّة *(iyya)* forms a singular feminine adjective, and the suffix يين *(iyyiin)* forms dual and plural (masculine and feminine) adjectives.

They are commonly used to indicate nationalities, with the country name (a noun) changed into a nationality (an adjective) as shown below.

☾ **Regular nouns (country names) with no long vowels**

The noun مَصْر (transliteration: *maṣr*; meaning: Egypt) forms adjectives to mean Egyptian as follows:

Masculine Singular	Feminine Singular	Dual / Plural (m. / f.)
مَصْرِي	مَصْرِيَّة	مَصْرِيِّين
maṣri	maṣriyya	maṣriyyiin

☾ **Nouns (country names) starting with the definite article (الـ)**

If the country name begins with the definite article الـ *(il)*, the definite article is dropped and a suffix is added.

The noun اليَمَن (transliteration: *ilyaman*; meaning: Yemen) forms adjectives to mean Yemeni as follows:

Masculine Singular	Feminine Singular	Dual / Plural (m. / f.)
يمنِي	يمَنِيَّة	يَمَنِيِّين
yamani	yamaniyya	yamaniyyiin

☾ **Nouns (country names) ending in ا (ʔalif)**

If the country name ends with an ا *(ʔalif)*, the ا is dropped and a suffix is added.

The noun أَمْرِيكا (transliteration: *ʔamriika;* meaning: America) forms adjectives to mean American as follows:

Masculine Singular	Feminine Singular	Dual / Plural (m. / f.)
أَمْرِيكِي	أَمْرِيكِيَّة	أَمْرِيكِيِّين
ʔamriiki	ʔamrikiyya	ʔamrikiyyiin

Nouns (country names) ending with ي (yaa)

If the country name ends with ي (yaa), the ي is dropped and a suffix is added.

The noun لِيبْيا (transliteration: *libyaa*; meaning: Libya) forms adjectives to mean Libyan as follows:

Masculine Singular	Feminine Singular	Dual / Plural (m. / f.)
لِيبِي	لِيبِيَّة	لِيبِيِّين
liibi	liibiyya	liibiyyiin

Exceptions

Country Name	Masculine Singular	Feminine Singular	Dual / Plural (m. / f.)
أَلْمَانِيا ʔalmanya Germany	أَلْمَانِي ʔalmaani	أَلْمَانِيَّة ʔalmaniyya	أَلْمَان ʔalmaan
فَرَنْسا faransa France	فَرَنْساوِي faransaawi	فَرَنْساوِيَّة faransaawiyya	فَرَنْساوِيِّين faransaawiyyiin
إِنْجِلْترا ʔengeltera England	إِنْجِلِيزِي ʔengeliizi	إِنْجِلِيزِيَّة ʔengeliiziyya	إِنْجِلِيز ʔengeliiz

الْهِنْد	هِنْدِي	هِنْدِيَّة	هُنُود
ilhend	hendi	hendiyya	hunuud
India			
تُونِس	تُونِسِي	تُونِسِيَّة	تَوَنْسا
tunis	tunisi	tunisiyya	tawansa
Tunisia			
الْمَغْرِب	مَغْرِبِي	مَغْرِبِيَّة	مَغارْبَة
ilmaɣrib	maɣribi	maɣribiyya	maɣarba
Morocco			

Other Uses of *Nisba* Adjectives

Nisba adjectives are not only used to form nationalities. They can also be used to change other nouns into adjectives.

For example, the nouns اقْتِصــاد (transliteration: *iqtiṣaad*; meaning: economy) and سِياسَة (transliteration: *siyaasa*; meaning: politics) form adjectives to mean economic and political as follows:

Noun	Masculine Adjective (s.)	Feminine Adjective (s.)	Dual / Plural Adjectives (m. / f.)
اقْتِصــاد	اقْتِصــادِي	اقْتِصــادِيَّة	اقْتِصــادِيِّين
iqtiṣaad	iqtiṣaadi	iqtiṣaadiyya	iqtiṣaadiyyiin
economy			
سِياسَة	سِياسِي	سِياسِيَّة	سِياسِيِّين
siyaasa	siyaasi	siyaasiyya	siyaasiyyiin
politics			

Exercise 1
Choose the correct adjective for each sentence.

Example:

هِيَّ (سُودانِي – سُودانِيَّة – سُودانِيِّين).

١- كرِسْتِين (مصري – أَلْمانِيَّة – فرنساويين).

٢- يوسِف وكمـال (تونِسِي – كويتِيَّة – قطَرِيِّين).

٣- إنْتِي (جزائري – مصْرِيَّة – سودانِيِّين).

٤- إحْنـا (أمْريكي – مـغربِيَّة – لِيبِيِّين).

٥- مُنَى (إنجْليزي – سعودِيَّة – هنُود).

٦- إنْتَ وهُوَّ (أسبانِي – هولَنْدِيَّة – يابانِيِّين).

٧- جـاك ومـايْكِل (سودانِي – مصرِيَّة – نرويجِيِّين).

٨- بَشَّـار (سوري – مـغربِيَّة – إيطالِيِّين).

٩- لارا (دنمـارْكِي – سويدِيَّة – إنجْليز).

١٠- سمِير (بحرينِي – لبنانِيَّة – ألمـان).

Exercise 2
Complete each sentence by forming adjectives (nationalities) from the country names provided.

Example:

البنـات _____ . (مَصْر)
البنـات مَصْرِيِّين.

١- إنْتِي _____ . (الـيَـابـان)

٢- هُمَّ _____ . (الـمَـكْسِيك)

٣- آدَم _____ . (فَرَنْسـا)

٤- لـيـلـى وَمـهـا _____ . (الـكَّـويت)

٥- سـمـير وكَـمـال _____ (قـطَر)

٦- سَـلْـوَى _____ . (إيطـالْيـا)

٧- نـوَّاف _____ (الـبـحْـرِين)

٨- هـالَـة _____ . (سُـورْيـا)

٩- الـجِّـيران دُول _____ . (لِـبْنـان)

١٠- إنتُـو _____ . (الـنِّـرْويـج)

Exercise 3
Fill in the correct forms of the adjectives provided.

Example:

إنْـتَ يُـونـانِـي.
هِـيَّ (يُـونـانِـيَّة)
هُـمَّ. (يُـونـانِـيِّـين)

١- هِـيَّ مَصْـرِيَّة.
هُـوَّ _____ .
هُـمَّ _____ .

٢- هُـمَّ لِـيـبِـيِّـين.
هُـوَّ _____ .
هِـيَّ _____ .

٣- هُوَّ فَرَنْسِي / فَرَنْساوِي.

هِيَّ _____ _____.

هُمَّ _____ _____.

٤- هِيَّ يَمَنِيَّة.

إِنْتُو _____ _____.

إِنْتَ _____.

٥- هُوّ فِلِسْطِينِي.

إِنْتِي _____.

إِحْنـا _____.

Exercise 4

Ask a classmate about his/her nationality (or nationalities) and then report to the rest of the class as in the example below.

Example:

إِنتِي مِنِين يا سـارَة؟

أنـا من أَمْرِيكـا.

سـارَة أمْرِيـكِـيَّـة.

Lesson 7: Possessive Adjectives

Possessive Pronouns

A possessive structure (noun + pronominal suffix) is used to express ownership and to clarify who or what a noun belongs to. The following table summarizes the pronominal suffixes that are attached to nouns and their corresponding transliterations.

English Possessive Pronouns	Arabic Pronominal Suffixes
his	ـه / ه u
her	ـها / ها ha
their (d./p.)	ـهُم / هُم hum
your (m.)	ـكَ ak
your (f.)	ـكِ ik
your (d./p.)	ـكُو / كُو ku
my	ـي i
our	ـنا / نا na

  Pronominal suffixes attached to masculine nouns
  Masculine nouns ending in one consonant
The following examples show how the appropriate pronominal suffixes are attached directly to nouns.

Possessive (English Translation)	كِتَاب ketaab
his book	كِتَابُه ketaabu
her book	كِتَابْهَا ketabha
their (d./p.) book	كِتَابْهُم ketabhum
your (m. s.) book	كِتَابَك ketaabak
your (f. s.) book	كِتَابِك ketaabik
your (d./p.) book	كِتَابْكُو ketabku
my book	كِتَابِي ketaabi
our book	كِتَابْنَا ketabna

Masculine nouns ending in two consonants

Three consonants in a row are not found in Arabic. When you have a masculine noun ending in two consonants, insert the following short vowels on the last consonant of the word before attaching the pronominal suffixes that begin with a consonant.

Suffix	Vowel	فَصْل faşl
هَا ha her	fatḥa a	فَصلَهَا faşlaha her classroom

هُم hum their (d./p.)	ḍamma u	فصـلـهم faṣluhum their classroom
كُو ku your (d./p.)	ḍamma u	فصـلـكو faṣluku your classroom
نا na our	kasra i	فصـلـنا faṣlina our classroom

In these cases, the short vowels are inserted on the last letter of the word فصل (on the letter ل), before the pronominal suffixes that begin with a consonant.

⤷ Pronominal suffixes attached to feminine nouns ending in ـة/ة (ta marbuuṭfa)

The final *ta marbuuṭfa* (the last consonant in the feminine noun, which you hear and pronounce as a short 'a') is changed to a regular ت *(t)*, and followed by the appropriate pronominal suffixes.

أجازة + ي ← أجـازْتـي	ʔagaaza + i → ʔagaazti	my vacation

If there are three consonants in a row, a *kasra* (short 'i') is inserted before the final *(t)*, and then the appropriate pronominal suffix is attached.

شَنْطَة + ها ← شَنْطِطْهـا	ʃanṭfa + ha → ʃanṭfitha	her bag

If the noun has the consonant ض *(ḍ)* followed by the consonant ت *(t)*, with no short vowel between them, this ضت *(ḍ + t)* is pronounced as a doubled ط *(ṭf)*, and then the appropriate pronominal suffix is attached.

أُوْضَة + ي ←يـ أُوْضَتِّي	ʔooḑa + i → ʔoʃʃī	my room

The following table summarizes the use of pronominal suffixes when attached to feminine nouns ending with ـة/ة *(ta marbuuṭa).*

	Feminine Noun	Exception 1*	Exception 2**
	مَكْتَبَة	شَنْطَة	أُوْضَة
	maktaba	ʃanṭa	ʔooḑa
	library/ bookcase	bag	room
his	مَكْتَبْتُه	شَنْطِتُه	أُوْضِتُّه
	maktabtu	ʃanṭitu	ʔoʃʃu
her	مَكْتَبِتْهَا	شَنْطِتْهَا	أُوْضِتْهَا
	maktabitha	ʃanṭitha	ʔoḑitha
their (d./p.)	مَكْتَبِتْهُم	شَنْطِتْهُم	أُوْضِتْهُم
	maktabithum	ʃanṭithum	ʔoḑithum
your (m. s.)	مَكْتَبْتَك	شَنْطِتَك	أُوْضِتَّك
	maktabtak	ʃanṭitak	ʔoʃʃak
your (f. s.)	مَكْتَبْتِك	شَنْطِتِك	أُوْضِتِّك
	maktabtik	ʃanṭitik	ʔoʃʃik
your (d./p.)	مَكْتَبِتْكُو	شَنْطِتْكُو	أُوْضِتْكُو
	maktabitku	ʃanṭitku	ʔoḑitku
my	مَكْتَبْتِي	شَنْطِتِي	أُوْضِتِّي
	maktabti	ʃanṭiti	ʔoʃʃī
our	مَكْتَبِتْنَا	شَنْطِتْنَا	أُوْضِتْنَا
	maktabitna	ʃanṭitna	ʔoḑitna

* Feminine nouns ending in three consonants
** Feminine nouns ending in ضة

☾ **Nouns ending in long vowels**

When the pronominal suffixes referring to the possessive pronouns 'my,' 'his,' and 'your' (s., m., and f.) are attached to masculine nouns ending with long vowels, a change in the pronunciation and the place of the vowel preceding the pronominal suffix takes place. The following table shows the form pronominal suffixes take when attached to nouns ending with long vowels.

	Noun Ending with ١	Noun Ending with و	Noun Ending with ي
	بـابـا	أَخّ/أَخُو	كُرْسِي
	baaba	?axx / ?axu	kursi
	father	brother	chair
his	بـابـاه	أَخُوه	كُرْسِـيـه
	babaah	?axuuh	kursiih
her	بـابـاهـا	أَخُوهـا	كُرْسِـيـهـا
	babaaha	?axuuha	kursiiha
their (d./p.)	بـابـاهُم	أَخُوهُم	كُرْسِـيـهُم
	babaahum	?axuuhum	kursiihum
your (m. s.)	بـابـاك	أَخُوك	كُرْسِـيـك
	babaak	?axuuk	kursiik
your (f. s.)	بـابـاكِي	أَخُوكِي	كُرْسِـيـكِي
	babaaki	?axuuki	kursiiki
your (d./p.)	بـابـاكُو	أَخُوكُو	كُرْسِـيـكُو
	babaaku	?axuuku	kursiiku
my	بـابـايـا	أَخُويـا	كُرْسِـيًّا
	babaaya	?axuuya	kursiyya
our	بـابـانـا	أَخُونـا	كُرْسِـينـا
	babaana	?axuuna	kursiina

Forming Possessive Structures with the "Belonging to" (بِتـاع) Structure

How to form the structure of بِتـاع *(bitaaʒ)*

A definite noun is followed by the correct form of بِتـاع *(bitaaʒ)* and another definite noun, as follows:

الْكِتـاب بِتـاع الْمُدَرِّس	ikketaab bitaaʒ-ilmudarris
the book belonging to the teacher / the teacher's book	

The structure can also be formed with a definite noun and the correct form of بِتـاع with a pronominal suffix, that is, a possessive.

الْكِتـاب بِتـاعُه	ikketaab bitaaʒu
the book belonging to him / his book	

If the first definite noun is masculine, the masculine form بِتـاع *(bitaaʒ)* is used.

الْبِيـت بِتـاع جِدِّي	ilbeet bitaaʒ giddi
the house belonging to my grandfather / my grandfather's house	

If the first definite noun is feminine or non-human plural, the feminine form بِتـاعِة *(bitaaʒit)* is used.

السَّاعَة بِتـاعِة الْبِنْت	issaaʒa bitaaʒit-ilbint
the watch belonging to the girl / the girl's watch	
الْكُتُب بِتـاعِة الْمُدَرِّس	ikkutub bitaaʒit-ilmudarris
the books belonging to the teacher / the teacher's book	

If the first definite noun is dual or plural, the plural form بِتُوع *(bituuʒ)* is used.

الْمُهَنْدِسِين بِتُوع الشِّرْكَة	ilmuhandesiin bituuʒ-iʃʃirka
the engineers belonging to the company / the company's engineers	

The following table shows the different forms of the structure of بِتاع when pronominal suffixes are attached.

		Masculine	Feminine	Dual and Plural
		بِتاع bitaaʒ	بِتاعة bitaaʒit	بِتُوع bituuʒ
his		بِتاعُه bitaaʒu	بِتاعْثُه bitaʒtu	بِتُوعُه bituuʒu
her		بِتاعْها bitaʒha	بِتاعِثْها bitaʒitha	بِتُوعْها bituʒha
their (d./p.)		بِتاعْهُم bitaʒhum	بِتاعِثْهُم bitaʒithum	بِتُوعْهُم bituʒhum
your (m. s.)		بِتاعَك bitaaʒak	بِتاعْتَك bitaʒtak	بِتُوعَك bituuʒak
your (f. s.)		بِتاعِك bitaaʒik	بِتاعْتِك bitaʒtik	بِتُوعِك bituuʒik
your (d./p.)		بِتاعْكُو bitaʒku	بِتاعِثْكُو bitaʒitku	بِتُوعْكُو bituʒku
my		بِتاعِي bitaaʒi	بِتاعْتِي bitaʒti	بِتُوعِي bituuʒi
our		بِتاعْنا bitaʒna	بِتاعِثْنا bitaʒitna	بِتُوعْنا bituʒna

When to use the structure بِتاع
This structure may be used with loanwords from other languages.

الرَّادْيُو بِتاعِي	irradyu bitaaʒi
the radio belonging to me / my radio	

The structure can also be used with nouns referring to people's professions or vocations.

الـمُحـامِي بِتـاعِي	ilmuḥaami bitaaʒi	my lawyer
الـدُكْتُور بِتـاعِي	idduktoor bitaaʒi	my doctor
البَوّاب بِتـاعِي	ilbawwaab bitaaʒi	my doorman

The structure بِتـاع, in all its forms, is never used with family members or parts of the body.

Exercise 1
Choose the correct translation for each sentence.

Example:
This is his shirt.
- دا قَمِيصُـه
- دا مِش قَمِيصُـه
- دا مِش قَمِيص بِتاعُـه

---

1. This is not her book.
- دا مِش كتـابْـهـا.
- دا مِش كتـاب بتـاعُـهـا.
- دا كتـابْـهـا.

2. These are your (f. s.) books.
- دِي كُتُب بِتـاعْتِك.
- دِي كُتُبِك.
- دِي الـكُـتُبِك.

3. Your (p.) friends are Lebanese.
- الأصـحـاب بِتُـوعَك لِبْنـانِيِّـين.
- الأصـحـابْـكُو لِبْنـانِيِّـين.
- أصْـحـابْـكُو لِبْنـانِيِّـين.

4. My teacher is Spanish.

- أُسْتـاذ بتـاعِـي أسبـانـي.
- الأُستـاذِي أسبـانـي.
- أستـاذِي أسبـانـي.

5. His dentist is British.

- دكتور بتـاع الأسنـان بـريطـانـي.
- دكتُور الأسْنـان بتـاعُـه بـريطـانـي.
- دكتـوري الأسنـان بـريطـانـي.

6. Their father is an engineer.

- أبـوهُم مُـهـنْـدِس.
- الأبوهُم مُـهـنْـدِس.
- الأبّ بتـاعُـهُم مُـهـنْـدِس.

7. Our house is on this street.

- بيتنـا فِي الشـارع دا.
- البيتنـا في الشـارع دا.
- بيت بتـاعْنـا في الشـارع دا.

8. Her music is beautiful.

- الموسيقِتْهـا جميـلـة.
- الموسيقـى بتـاعِتْهـا جميـلـة.
- موسيقى بتـاعِتْهـا جميـلـة.

9. Our doorman is kind.

- بَوّاب بتـاعْنـا طَيِّب.
- البـوابنـا طَيِّب.
- البَوّاب بتـاعْنـا طَيِّب.

10. When is his holiday?

- أجـازْتُـه إمْتَـى؟
- أجـازَة بتـاعتُـه إمتَـى؟
- الأجـازْتُـه إمتَـى؟

Exercise 2

Complete each sentence by attaching the correct pronominal suffix to the noun provided.

Example:

ـ فِين (جامْعة + هُوَّ)؟ ← فِين جامْعِتُه؟

١ـ دا (بِيت + إحْنا) _____ .

٢ـ (أُسْتاذ + إنْتُو) _____ ساكِن فِي الشَّارِع دا.

٣ـ (جار + هُوَّ) _____ لِبْنانِي.

٤ـ (أُخْت + أنا) _____ طالِبَة.

٥ـ (كِتاب + إنْتِي) _____ عَ المَكْتَب.

٦ـ (مُديرَة + هُمَّ) _____ أَمْريكِيَّة.

٧ـ (دَرْس + إنْتَ) _____ السَّاعَة كام؟

٨ـ (ماما + هِيَّ) _____ مُوَظَّفَة فِي البَنْك دا.

٩ـ (أخّ + إنْتِي) _____ فِي جامْعِة إيه؟

١٠ـ (شَقَّة + هُمَّ) _____ هِنا.

Exercise 3

Complete each sentence using the correct form of بِتاع and the noun provided.

Example:

ـ (فُسْتان + هِيَّ) _____ فِي الدُّولاب. ← الفُسْتان بِتاعْها فِي الدُّولاب.

١- دا (كُمْبِيوتَر + إِنْتِي) _____.

٢- هِيَّ (مُدِيرَة + أَنـا) _____.

٣- دِي (كُتُب + هِيَّ) _____.

٤- (مُحـامِي + إِحْنـا) _____ سـاكِن هِنـا.

٥- (راديو + إِنْتُو) _____ مِش عَ المَكْتَب.

٦- (شَقَّة + هُمَّ) _____ هِنـا.

٧- دِي (قُمْصـان + هُوَّ) _____.

٨- دِي (جـامْعَـة + إِنْتَ) _____.

٩- (نـادِي + أَنـا) _____ فـي الشّـارِع دا.

١٠- دا (بِيـانُـو + هِـيَّ) _____.

Exercise 4

Talk about your family and ask your classmates about their families. Report what they said to the rest of the class. Make sure to use the correct pronominal suffixes attached to nouns and the بتـاع structure (as applicable).

Lesson 8: Possessive Nouns

The possessive إضافة *(ʔiḍafa)* is another structure that is employed to express ownership and to clarify who or what a noun belongs to.

Formation of the *ʔiḍafa* Construction
◟ **Adding a pronominal suffix**
ʔiḍafa can be formed by adding a pronominal suffix to a noun, as was explained in lesson 7.

كِتـاب + ي ← كِتـابِي	ketaab + i → ketaabi	my book

◟ **Adding a noun to another noun**
ʔiḍafa can also be formed by adding a noun to another noun. In this case, the possessed object occurs before the one possessing this object.

The possessed object (the first noun of the *ʔiḍafa* construction) should always remain indefinite (meaning it does not begin with الـ) whereas the one possessing the object (the second noun of the *ʔiḍafa* construction) can be either definite or indefinite.

كِتـاب وَلَد	ketaab walad	a boy's book
كِتـاب الـوَلَد	ketaab ilwalad	the boy's book
مَكْتَبِين هُـدَى	maktabeen huda	Huda's two offices
مُـدَرِّسِين آدم	mudarrisiin ʔaadam	Adam's teachers

Several Arabic *ʔiḍafa* constructions might occur as one unit in an Arabic sentence.

دا كِتـاب مُدَرِّس بِنْت أُخْتِـي	da ketaab mudarris bint-u-xti
This is the book of the teacher of my niece (literally: the daughter of my sister) / my niece's teacher's book	

Four *ʔiḍafa* constructions occurred in this example:
1. كِتـاب مُدَرِّس a teacher's book
2. مُدَرِّس بِنْت a girl's teacher

3. بِنْت أُخْت a sister's girl
4. أُخْتِي (أُخْت + أَنـا) my sister

    As you will notice, كِتـاب – مُدَرِّس – بِنْت – اخت are indefinite because each one of them functions as the first noun of the Arabic *ʔiḍafa* construction (the possessed object), which should always remain indefinite.

Exercise 1
Mark each sentence as correct or incorrect, and rewrite those that are incorrect

Example:

الشَّنْطَة الطَّالِب عَلَى الْمَكْتَب. (X)
شَنْطِة الطَّالِب عَلَى الْمَكْتَب.

١ـ البيت المـدِير فِي القـاهِرة.

_____

٢ـ شَقِة الأستـاذ هِنـا.

_____

٣ـ دا الكتـاب الطـالِب.

_____

٤ـ أنـا الأخـت المـدرّسَة.

_____

٥ـ حفلِة الجـامْعـة بكُرَة.

_____

٦ـ أتُوبِيس الجـامْعَـة مِش قدّام المكتبـة.

_____

٧ـ القَمِـيص الـولـد بكـام؟

_____

٨ـ فِين عنوان البيت؟

_____

٩ـ دِي النضارة الطالبة الأمريكِيَّة.

_____

١٠ـ عايِز عَصِير لِمُون.

_____

> **Exercise 2**
> Translate each sentence using the *ʔiḍafa* construction.

Example:

This is the school's bus.

دا أتُوبِيس/باص الْمَدْرَسَة.

_____

1. This is a teacher's office.

_____

2. The doctor's room is here.

_____

3. Adam's chair is not here.

_____

4. She is Maha's teacher.

_____

5. Here is the door of his house.

_____

6. The woman's computer is not here.

_____

7. This is a swimming pool.

_____

8. This is our classroom's window.

_____

9. These are Maha's two books.

_____

10. This is the lawyer's house.

_____

> **Exercise 3**
> Use two or more words from the box below to form *ʔiḍafa*
> constructions and then put each *ʔiḍafa* into a full sentence.

Example:

صـاحِب – بِيت
صـاحِب الـبِيت سُورِي.

جامْـعَة – بِيت – عِيلـة – أُسْتـاذ – فُسْتـان – هُمَّ – فَصْـل – شِرْكَـة – شـارِع – شَقَّـة – مُدِير – مَصْر – هِـيَّ – كُتُب – اِبْن – جِدّ – إِنْتِي – بـابـا – مَكْتَبَـة – أُخْـت – شـارِع – بَذْلَة – بـوّاب – جـار – صـاحِب – عِمـارَة

Lesson 9: Prepositions

Prepositions Connoting Possession

In addition to their functions as prepositions (حروف جرّ), some Arabic prepositions function as the verb 'to have.' Among these are the following:

عَنْد	مَعَ	لِـ	قُدَّام	وَرا	عَلـى
ʒand	maʒa	li	ʔuddaam	wara	ʒala
at the place of	with	for/to	in front of	behind	on

To function as the verb 'to have,' these prepositions must have a pronominal suffix of possession attached and/or be followed by an indefinite noun.

عَنْد + pronominal suffix or noun

عَنْد is a preposition that means 'at the place of.' It functions as the verb 'to have' when referring to property, children, disease, age, responsibilities, and tasks, as follows:

Anything one possesses (property)

عَنْدُه شَقَّة واسْعَة.	ʒandu ʃaʔʔa wasʒa	He has a big apartment.

Children

عَنْدِي أوْلاد.	ʒandi ʔawlaad	I have children.

Symptoms or disease

عَنْدِي صُداع.	ʒandi ṣuḍaaʒ	I have a headache.
عَنْدِي بَرْد.	ʒandi bard	I have a cold.

Age

عَنْدُه خَمَسْتـاشَر (١٥) سَنَة.	ʒandu xamastaaʃar sana	He's fifteen years old.

Responsibilities or tasks one has to perform/do

عَنْدِي اِمْتِحـان بُكْرَة.	ʒandi-imtħaan bukra	I have an exam tomorrow.

مَعَ + pronominal suffix or noun

مع is a preposition that means 'with.' It can function as the verb 'to have' when referring to something that a person has at present.

Something with a person now, at the moment of speaking

مَعـاك فُلـوس؟	maʒaak fuluus	Do you have money?
أَيْـوَه مَعـايـا.	ʔaywa maʒaaya	Yes, I do (have it).

لِ + pronominal suffix or noun

لِ is a preposition that means 'for' or 'to.' It can function as the verb 'to have,' especially when referring to debts or to emotional moods and feelings, as follows:

There is/are ('for' someone)

لِـيهُم قَرايِب كِتـير فِي إِسْكِنْدِرِيَّة.	liihum ʔaraayib kitiir f-iskindiriyya	They have lots of relatives in Alexandria.
لِيَّه جَوابات النَّهـارْدَه؟	liyya gawabaat-nahaarda	Do I have any letters today? / Are there letters for me today?
أَيْـوَه لِيك / لِيكِي.	ʔaywa liik / liiki	Yes, you have. / Yes, there are.

لِيـهـا فلـوس عَنـدَك.	liiha fuluus ʒandak	You owe her money.

Moods

لِيّـه مَزاج أرُوح السِّيـنِـما.	liyya mazaag-aruuħ-issinima	I feel like going to the cinema.

قُدَّام + pronominal suffix or noun

قُدَّام is a preposition that means 'in front of.' It can function as the verb 'to have' when referring to things one could possess (in the future) or the time one has before something happens, as follows:

Being on the horizon (in the future)

قُدَّامُـه وَظِـيـفَـة كُوَيِّسـة.	ʔuddaamu waziifa-kuwayyisa	There is a good job before him / He has a good job in store for him.
عـايِـز شَـقَّة! أنَا قُدَّامِـي شَـقَّة كُوَيِّسَـة لُـه.	ʒaayiz ʃaʔʔa ʔana ʔuddaami ʃaʔʔa-kuwayyisa luh	He wants an apartment! I have a good one for him.

Time ahead of someone

قُدَّامِـي ست شُـهُور واتخَـرَّج.	ʔuddaami sitti-ʃhuur watxarrag	I have six months to go before I graduate.

وَرا + pronominal suffix or noun

وَرا is a preposition that means 'behind.' It can function as the verb 'to have' when referring to the tasks one has to do, as follows:

Things one has to do

وَراهُـم واجِـبات كِـتِـير دِلوَقْـتِـي.	waraahum wagibaat kitiir dilwaʔti	They have lots of homework now.

عَلـَى +pronominal suffix or noun

عَلـَى is a preposition that means 'on.' It can function as the verb 'to have' when referring to responsibilities and debts, as follows:

◉ **A responsibility or burden**

عَلِيكُو واجِبـات كتِير لِبُكْرَه.	ʒaleeku wagibaat kitiir libukra	You have a lot of assignments for tomorrow.

◉ **Owing someone (debt)**

عَلَيَّه فُلُوس لِلمُدِير.	ʒalayya fuluus lilmudiir	I owe the director money.

◉ **Body parts**

The English structure of (pronoun + has/have + adjective + body part) changes in Egyptian Colloquial Arabic to (body part + pronominal suffix + adjective). To give the English meaning of "she has long hair" in Arabic, for example, one says "her hair is long." Similarly, "he has blue eyes" becomes "his eyes are blue."

شَـعْرَهـا طَـوِيل.	ʃaʒraha ʧawiil	She has long hair.
عِينِيه زُرْق.	ʒineeh zurʔ	He has blue eyes.

◉ **Engagement and marriage**

To give the equivalent of the English meaning "he has a wife" or "she has a husband," in Egyptian Colloquial Arabic, a person's marital status is described through the (pronoun + verb to be + status) structure and not the (pronoun + have/has + partner) structure. Thus, the English "he has a wife" or "she has a husband," becomes "he/she is married" and "he/she has a fiancé(e)" becomes "he/she is engaged."

هُـوَّ مِـتْجَـوِّز.	huwwa mitgawwiz	He is married.
هِـيَّ مِـتْجَـوِّزَة.	heyya mitgawwiza	She is married.

هُوَّ خاطِب.	huwwa xaaʧib	He is engaged.
هِيَّ مَخْطُوبَة.	heyya maxʧuuba	She is engaged.

↳ Negating

When the above-mentioned prepositions have pronominal suffixes, they can be negated with a prefix مَ *(ma)* and a suffix ش *(ʃ)*.

The following tables show the prepositions with attached pronominal suffixes.

▭ Negative + عَنْد

عَنْد	ʒand	at the place of
Personal Pronoun	**Affirmative Form**	**Negative Form**
هُوَّ huwwa he	عَنْدُه ʒandu	مَعَنْدُوش maʒanduuʃ
هِيَّ heyya she	عَنْدَها ʒandaha	مَعَنْدَهاش maʒandahaaʃ
هُمَّ humma they (d./p.)	عَنْدُهُم ʒanduhum	مَعَنْدُهُمْش maʒanduhumʃ
إِنْتَ ʔenta you (m. s.)	عَنْدَك ʒandak	مَعَنْدَكْش maʒandakʃ
إِنْتِي ʔenti you (f. s.)	عَنْدِك ʒandik	مَعَنْدِكِيش maʒandikiiʃ
إِنْتُو ʔentu you (d./p.)	عَنْدُكُو ʒanduku	مَعَنْدُكُوش maʒandukuuʃ

أنَا ʔana I	عَنْدِي ʒandi	مَعَنْدِيش maʒandiiʃ
إِحْنَا ʔeħna we	عَنْدِنَا ʒandena	مَعَنْدِنَاش maʒandenaaʃ

▨ Negative + مع

مَعَ	maʒa	with
Personal Pronoun	**Affirmative Form**	**Negative Forms**
هُوَّ huwwa he	مَعَاه maʒaah	مَعَهُوش / مَمْعَهُوش maʒahuuʃ / mamʒahuuʃ
هِيَّ heyya she	مَعَاهَا maʒaaha	مَعَهَاش / مَمْعَهَاش maʒahaaʃ / mamʒahaaʃ
هُمَّ humma they (d./p.)	مَعَاهُم maʒaahum	مَعَهُمْش / مَمْعَهُمْش maʒahumʃ / mamʒahumʃ
إِنْتَ ʔenta you (m. s.)	مَعَاك maʒaak	مَعَكْش / مَمْعَكْش maʒakʃ / mamʒakʃ
إِنْتِي ʔenti you (f. s.)	مَعَاكي maʒaaki	مَعَكِيش / مَمْعَكِيش maʒakiiʃ / mamʒakiiʃ

Personal Pronoun	Affirmative Form	Negative Forms
إنْتُو ?entu you (d./p.)	مَعاكُو maʒaaku	مَعَكُوش / مَمْعَكُوش maʒakuuʃ / mamʒakuuʃ
أنا ?ana I	مَعايا maʒaaya	مَعِييش / مَمْعِييش maʒyiiʃ / mamʒayiiʃ
إحْنا ?eħna we	مَعانا maʒaana	مَعْناش / مَمْعَناش maʒanaaʃ / mamʒanaaʃ

▤ Negative + لـ

لـ	li	for/to
Personal Pronoun	**Affirmative Form**	**Negative Forms**
هُوَّ huwwa he	لِيه liih	مَلُوش / مَلْهُوش maluuʃ / malhuuʃ
هِيَّ heyya she	لِيها liiha	مَلْهاش malhaaʃ
هُمَّ humma they (d./p.)	لِيهُم liihum	مَلْهُمْش malhumʃ
إنْتَ ?enta you (m. s.)	لِيك liik	مَلَكْش malakʃ
إنْتِي ?enti you (f. s.)	لِيكِي liiki	مَلْكِيش malkiiʃ

إِنْتُو ʔentu you (d./p.)	لِيكُو liiku	مَلْكُوش malkuuʃ
أنا ʔana I	لِيَّه liyya	مَلِيش maliiʃ
إِحْنا ʔeħna we	لِينا liina	مَلْناش malnaaʃ

Negative + قُدَّام

قُدَّام	ʔuddaam	in front of
Personal Pronoun	Affirmative Form	Negative Form
هُوَّ huwwa he	قُدَّامُه ʔuddaamu	مـاقُدَّامُوش maʔuddamuuʃ
هِيَّ heyya she	قُدَّامْها ʔuddamha	مـاقُدَّامْهـاش maʔuddamhaaʃ
هُمَّ humma they (d./p.)	قُدَّامْهُم ʔuddamhum	مـاقُدَّامْهُمْش maʔuddamhumʃ
إِنْتَ ʔenta you (m. s.)	قُدَّامَك ʔuddaamak	مـاقُدَّامَكْش maʔuddamakʃ
إِنْتِي ʔenti you (f. s.)	قُدَّامِك ʔuddaamik	مـاقُدَّامْكِيش maʔuddamkiiʃ

إنْتُو	قُدَّامْكُو	مـاقُدَّامْكُوش
?entu	?uddamku	ma?uddamkuuʃ
you (d./p.)		

أنـا	قُدَّامِي	مـاقُدَّامِيش
?ana	?uddaami	ma?uddamiiʃ
I		

إحْنـا	قُدَّامْنـا	مـاقُدَّامْنـاش
?eħna	?uddamna	ma?uddamnaaʃ
we		

🔊 **Negative + ورا**

وَرا	wara	behind
Personal Pronoun	**Affirmative Form**	**Negative Form**
هُوَّ	وَراه	مَوَراهُوش
huwwa	waraah	mawarahuuʃ
he		
هِيَّ	وَراهـا	مَوَراهـاش
heyya	waraaha	mawarahaaʃ
she		
هُمَّ	وَراهُم	مَوَراهُمـش
humma	waraahum	mawarahumʃ
they (d./p.)		
إنْتَ	وَراك	مَوَرَكْش
?enta	waraak	mawarakʃ
you (m. s.)		
إنْتِـي	وَراكِـي	مَوَراكِيش
?enti	waraaki	mawarakiiʃ
you (f. s.)		

إِنْتُو ʔentu you (d./p.)	وَراكُو waraaku	مَوَراكُوش mawarakuuʃ
أَنـا ʔana I	وَرايـا waraaya	مَوَرايِيش mawarayiiʃ
إِحْنـا ʔeħna we	وَرانـا waraana	مَوَرانـاش mawaranaaʃ

Negative + على

عَلَى 	ʒala	on
Personal Pronoun	**Affirmative Form**	**Negative Form**
هُوَّ huwwa he	عَليـه ʒaleeh	مَعَليـهُوش maʒalihuuʃ
هِيَّ heyya she	عَليـها ʒaleeha	مَعَليـهاش maʒalihaaʃ
هُمَّ humma they (d./p.)	عَليـهُم ʒaleehum	مَعَليـهُمْش maʒalihumʃ
إِنْتَ ʔenta you (m. s.)	عَليك ʒaleek	مَعَلِكْش maʒalikʃ
إِنْتـي ʔenti you (f. s.)	عَليـكـي ʒaleeki	مَعَلِكِيش maʒalikiiʃ

إِنْتُو	عَلِيكُو	مَعَلِيكُوش
?entu	ʒaleeku	maʒalikuuʃ
you (d./p.)		
أَنَا	عَلَيَّا	مَعَلِيَّاش
?ana	ʒalayya	maʒaliyyaaʃ
I		
إِحْنَا	عَلِينَا	مَعَلِنَاش
?eḥna	ʒaleena	maʒalinaaʃ
we		

Prepositions that Do Not Mean "to Have"

There are other prepositions that do not carry the meaning of the verb 'to have.' These are shown in the following table.

فِي	fi	in
بِ	bi	with
قَبْل	?abl	before
بَعْد	baʒd	after
مِن	min	from
عَن	ʒan	about / on
جَنْب	gamb	next to

The following tables show these prepositions with attached pronouns. Note that فِي has both affirmative and negative forms.

فِي	fi	in
Personal Pronoun	**Affirmative Form**	**Negative Form**
هُوَّ huwwa he	فِيه fiih	مَفِيهُوش mafihuuʃ
هِيَّ heyya she	فِيهَا fiiha	مَفِيهَاش mafihaaʃ
هُمَّ humma they (d./p.)	فِيهُم fiihum	مَفِيهُمْش mafihumʃ
إِنْتَ ʔenta you (m. s.)	فِيك fiik	مَفِكْش mafikʃ
إِنْتِي ʔenti you (f. s.)	فِيكِي fiiki	مَفِيكِيش mafikiiʃ
إِنْتُو ʔentu you (d./p.)	فِيكُو fiiku	مَفِيكُوش mafikuuʃ
أَنَا ʔana I	فِيَّه fiyya	مَفِيَّاش mafiyyaaʃ
إِحْنَا ʔeḥna we	فِينَا fiina	مَفِينَاش mafinaaʃ

Personal Pronoun	Preposition		
	بِـ bi with	قَبْل ʔabl before	بَعْد baʒd after
هُوَّ huwwa he	بِيه biih	قَبْلُه ʔablu	بَعْدُه baʒdu
هِيَّ heyya she	بِيها biiha	قَبْلْها ʔablaha	بَعْدَها baʒdaha
هُمَّ humma they (d./p.)	بِيهُم biihum	قَبْلْهُم ʔabluhum	بَعْدْهُم baʒduhum
إِنْتَ ʔenta you (m. s.)	بِيك biik	قَبْلَك ʔablak	بَعْدَك baʒdak
إِنْتِي ʔenti you (f. s.)	بِيكِي biiki	قَبْلِك ʔablik	بَعْدِك baʒdik
إِنْتُو ʔentu you (d./p.)	بِيكُو biiku	قَبْلْكُو ʔabluku	بَعْدْكُو baʒduku
أَنا ʔana I	بِيَّه biyya	قَبْلِي ʔabli	بَعْدِي baʒdi
إِحْنا ʔeħna we	بِينا biina	قَبْلْنا ʔablina	بَعْدْنا baʒdina

Some forms of the following have two possible pronunciations.

Personal Pronoun	Preposition	
	مِن min from	عَن ʒan about / on
هُوَّ huwwa he	مِنُّه minnu	عَنُّه ʒannu
هِيَّ heyya she	مِنْها / مِنَّها minnaha / minha	عَنْها / عَنَّها ʒannaha / ʒanha
هُمَّ humma they (d./p.)	مِنْهُم / مِنُّهُم minnuhum / minhum	عَنْهُم / عَنُّهُم ʒannuhum / ʒanhum
إِنْتَ ʔenta you (m. s.)	مِنَّك minnak	عَنَّك ʒannak
إِنْتِي ʔenti you (f. s.)	مِنَّك minnik	عَنَّك ʒannik
إِنْتُو ʔentu you (d./p.)	مِنْكُو / مِنُّكُو minnuku / minku	عَنْكُو / عَنُّكُو ʒannuku / ʒanku
أنا ʔana I	مِنِّي minni	عَنِّي ʒanni

إِحْنا	مِنّا / مِنّنا	عَنّا / عَنّنا
?eħna	minnina / minna	ʒannina / ʒanna
we		

If a word has the consonant ن *(n)* followed by the consonant ب *(b)*, with no short vowel breaking them, the ن *(n)* is pronounced as an م *(m)*. This is shown in the following table with جَـنْـب (which is pronounced *gamb*).

Personal Pronoun	Preposition
	جَنْب
	gamb
	next to
هُوَّ	جَنْبُه
huwwa	gambu
he	
هِيَّ	جَنْبَها
heyya	gambaha
she	
هُمَّ	جَنْبُهُم
humma	gambuhum
they (d./p.)	
إِنْتَ	جَنْبَك
?enta	gambak
you (m. s.)	
إِنْتِي	جَنْبِك
?enti	gambik
you (f. s.)	

إِنْتُو ʔentu you (d./p.)	جَنْبُكُو gambuku
أَنَا ʔana I	جَنْبِي gambi
إِحْنَا ʔeħna we	جَنْبِنَا gambina

Other Prepositions

Preposition	Transliterated Form	English Translation
تَحْت	taħt	under, below, downstairs, beneath
فُوق	fooʔ	above, on top of, upstairs
جُوَّه	guwwa	inside, in
بَرَّه	barra	outside, out
هِنَا	hena	here
هِنَاك	henaak	there
بِين	been	between, among
قُصَاد	ʔuṣaad	in front of, opposite
نَاحِيِة	naħyit	toward
حَوَالِين	ħawaleen	around (surrounding)

Exercise 1
Choose the correct preposition for each sentence.

Example:

يُوسِف ____ شُغْل كِتير النَّهارْدَه.
(عَنْدُه – مَعاه – فِيه)

١- ليلى _____ فرصة شغل ممتازة في الإمارات.
(وراها – قدَّامها – عَنْدَها)

٢- إحنا _____ أكل كفاية للرحلة.
(مَمْعناش – مَعَلِناش – ماوراناش)

٣- بيتي _____ سوبر ماركت.
(مَمْعَهوش – ماجنبوش – مَعَلِيهُوش)

٤- سامِي _____ أولاد.
(ماوراهوش – معندوش – ماقُدَّامُوش)

٥- الصحرا _____ مَيَّه.
(مَفِيهاش – مَعَلِيهاش – مَمْعَهاش)

٦- قرايبي _____ شركة كبيرة.
(مَعاهم – عندهم – فِيهُم)

٧- إنتَ _____ مشاوير دلوقتي؟
(معاك – وراك – فِيك)

٨- اِتفضَّلي عَصِير. لأ _____ نِفْس.
(مَعَلِيَّاش – مَلِيش – مَفِيّاش)

٩- _____ حساب في بنك "باركليز"؟
(وراك – عَنْدَك – مَعاك)

١٠- _____ ٥٠ جِنِيه عند سَلْوَى.
(لِيه – قُدَّامُه – وراه)

Exercise 2
Translate each sentence into Arabic.

Example:
The teacher is in the university.

الأُسْـتـاذ فِي الـجَّـامْـعَـة.

1. The girl is behind the tree.

_____

2. The ball is under the table.

_____

3. The man and the woman are in front of the television.

_____

4. The chair is next to the bed.

_____

5. The book is on the desk.

_____

6. The boy is on the street.

_____

7. The students are outside the classroom.

_____

8. The dictionary is with the girl.

_____

9. Cheese and bread are at the grocery store.

_____

10. Trees are around the house.

_____

Example:

جَنبَها جامْعَة. (إحْنـا)
جَنبِنـا جـامْعَة.

١- مـعـايـا سَندويتْشـات كِتِير. (هُمَّ)

٢- عَنـدَك كُتُـب. (هُوَّ)

٣- قُدَّامُـه أوْراق. (أنـا)

٤- مَعـانـا قـامُوس. (هُوَّ)

٥- عَنْدُه موبـايِـل. (إنْتِـي)

٦- الـتَّرابِيزَة عَلِيهـا قَلَم. (المَكْتَب)

٧- الـبـاب لُـه مُفْتـاح. (الشَّقَّة)

٨- لَيْلَى جَنبَها نـادِي. (إنْتُـو)

٩- الأوْضَـة فِيهـا كَراسِـي. (الـبِيت)

١٠- بِيت لَيْلَى وَراه مَحَطَّةُ أوتُوبِيس. (الـجَـامْعَة)

Exercise 4
Negate each of the following sentences.

Example:

قُدامُه كُتُب كِتِيرَة.
ماقُدامُوش كُتُب كِتِيرَة.

١- عَنْدِي دَرْس دِلْوَقْتِي.

_____

٢- شَقَّتِي قُدَّامُها عِيادةْ دُكْتُور.

_____

٣- لِيكُو أَوْراق فِي المَكْتَب.

_____

٤- مَعانا عَصِير بُرْتُقان.

_____

٥- البِيت فِيه تِليفِزْيُون.

_____

٦- عَلِينا واجِبات كِتِير.

_____

٧- مَعاهُم فِي العَمَارَة جَارَة سُورِيَّة.

_____

٨- قُدَّامِك مَرْكَز لُغات.

_____

٩- وَراك مِشْوار.

_____

١٠- عَنْدُكُو شُغْل دِلْوَقْتِي.

_____

Lesson 10: Dual and Plural Nouns

Dual (الـمـثـنـى) Nouns

To make the dual form from a masculine noun, add the suffix ين *(een)*.

كِتـاب	ketaab	book
كِتـابـيـن	ketabeen	two books

If the noun is feminine and ends with a ة / ـة *(ta marbuutʃa)*, when written, change the ة / ـة to a regular ت *(t)* and then add the suffix ين *(een)*.

شَنْطَة	ʃanʃa	bag
شَنْطِتِـين	ʃanʃiteen	two bags

If the noun is feminine but does not end with a ة / ـة *(ta marbuutʃa)*, add the suffix يـن *(een)*.

بِنْت	bint	girl
بِنْتِـيـن	binteen	two girls

⟳ **Exception**

سِتّ	sitt	woman
اتْنِـيـن سِتّـات	itneen sittaat	two women

Plural (الـجـمـع) Nouns
⟳ **Masculine nouns**

Some masculine plural nouns are formed by adding the suffix يـن *(iin)* to the singular form.

مُـدَرِّس	mudarris	teacher
مُـدَرِّسـيـن	mudarrisiin	teachers

However, most masculine nouns in Egyptian Colloquial Arabic have broken plurals (جمع تكسير) that should be memorized. The chart below shows some broken plural nouns.

Singular	Broken Plural	English Meaning
طَـالِب ʧaalib	طَـلَـبَة ʧalaba	student(s)
وَلَد walad	أوْلَاد / وِلَاد ʔawlaad / wilaad	boy(s) / child(ren)
أُسْـتَـاذ ʔustaaz	أسـاتْـذَة ʔasatza	teacher(s)
راجِل raagil	رِجَّـالَة riggaala	man (men)
خَـال xaal	أخـوال / خِيـلَان axwaal / xilaan	maternal uncle(s)
عَمّ ʒamm	أعمـام / عِمـام ʔaʒmaam / ʒimaam	paternal uncle(s)
صَـاحِـب ṣaaħib	أصْـحَاب / صُحَاب ʔaṣħaab / ṣuħaab	friend(s)
شَـارِع ʃaariʒ	شَـوارِع ʃawaariʒ	street(s)
بَنْك bank	بُنُوك bunuuk	bank(s)
قَلَم ʔalam	قِلَام ʔilaam	pen(s)
مَكْتَب maktab	مَكـاتِب makaatib	desk(s)
بِيت beet	بِيُوت biyuut	house(s) / home(s)

دَرْس dars	دُرُوس duruus	lesson(s)
كِتاب ketaab	كُتُب kutub	book(s)
كُرْسِي kursi	كَراسِي karaasi	chair(s)

▨ Exception

There are some masculine singular nouns which take the feminine plural form. These should be memorized.

Masculine Singular	Feminine Broken Plural	English Meaning
جَواب gawaab	جَوابات gawabaat	letter(s)
مِنَبِّه minabbih	مِنَبِّهـات minabbihaat	alarm clock(s)
شُـراب / شَـراب ʃuraab / ʃaraab	شُرابات / شَرابات ʃurabaat / ʃarabaat	sock(s)

↳ Feminine nouns

To form the plural of feminine nouns that end in ة / ـة *(ta marbuuʈa)*, drop the ة / ـة and add the suffix ات *(aat)*.

جـامْعَة	gamʒa	university
جـامْعـات	gamʒaat	universities

Most loanwords take the ات *(aat)* suffix in the plural.

تـاكْسِي	taksi	taxi
تـاكْسِيَّـات	taksiyyaat	taxis

Exception

Some feminine singular nouns have feminine broken plurals that should be memorized.

Feminine Singular	Feminine Broken Plural	English Meaning
مَدْرَسَة madrasa	مَدارِس madaaris	school(s)
أُوضَـة ʔooḍa	أُوَض ʔowaḍ	room(s)
شَقَّـة ʃaʔʔa	شُقَق ʃuʔaʔ	apartment(s)
قِزازَة ʔizaaza	قَزايِز ʔazaayiz	bottle(s)

Exercise 1

Mark each sentence as correct or incorrect, and rewrite those that are incorrect.

Example:

قُدَّامِـي خَمَس شَقَّـة. (X)
قُدَّامِـي خَمَس **شُقَق**.

_____

١. هِنـا فيـه بـيـتين.

_____

٢. عنـدِي قـمِـيصِـيـن.

_____

٣. يُـوسـف عنـده أربـع صـاحـبـيـن.

_____

٤. قُـدّام الـبـنـك مطـعـمـيـن كُبـار.

_____

٥. قدّام الجـامـعـة سِتِّين.

_____

٦. هنـاك عشَـر راجِل.

_____

٧. مَعَنـدِهـاش هُدُوم جـديـدة.

_____

٨. عندهـا تلـت عربـيـة جـديـدة.

_____

٩. عـايـز قزازتِيـن مِيَّة.

_____

١٠. شـقتِك فيـهـا أربـع أوضـة.

_____

Exercise 2
Change each sentence into the dual and into the plural.

Example:

دا بِـيـت.
دُول بِـيـتِـين / دِي بِـيُوت.

_____

١- هِـيَّ طـالِـبَـة.

_____

٢- دا قَـلَـم.

_____

٣- إِنْـتِـي أُسْـتـاذَة.

_____

٤- دِي ساعَة.

_____

٥- الشَّنْطَة هِنـاك.

_____

٦- فِيـه دَرْس النَّهـارْدَه.

_____

٧- دِي سِتّ.

_____

٨- البِنْت هِنـا.

_____

٩- دا مِش مُهَنْدِس.

_____

١٠- الْوَلَد مَصْرِي.

_____

Lesson 11: Adjectives, Comparatives, and Superlatives

Forms of Adjectives (الصفة)
In Egyptian Colloquial Arabic, adjectives occur after nouns to
describe and define these nouns. These adjectives should agree with
nouns they describe in gender and number. For example, a masculine
singular noun is described by a masculine singular adjective, and a
feminine singular noun is described by a feminine singular adjective.
Both masculine and feminine dual and plural human nouns are
described by plural adjectives. However, non-human plural nouns are
described by feminine singular adjectives.

Comparative and superlative adjectives in Egyptian Colloquial
Arabic have only one form (as shown in the following table) that is
used for masculine and feminine singular, dual, and human and non-
human plural forms. These should be memorized.

English Translation	Masculine	Feminine	Dual, Plural	Comparative, Superlative
small	صـغـيَّر ṣuɣayyar	صـغـيَّرة ṣuɣayyara	صـغـيَّرِين ṣuɣayyariin	أصـغـر ʔaṣɣar
few	قـلـيِّل ʔulayyil	قـلـيِّلة ʔulayyila	قـلـيِّلـين ʔulayyiliin	أقَلّ ʔaʔall
near	قـريِّب ʔurayyib	قـريِّبـة ʔurayyiba	قـريِّبـين ʔurayyibiin	أقرَب ʔaʔrab
high	عـالِي ʒaali	عـالية ʒalya	عـالِيين ʒalyiin	أعْلَى ʔaʒla

low	واطِي waaṭʃi	واطْيَة waṭʃya	واطْيِين waṭʃyiin	أوْطَى ʔawṭʃa
nice / sweet	حِلْو ħilw	حِلْوَة ħilwa	حِلْوِين ħilwiin	أحْلَى ʔaħla
expensive	غالِي ɣaali	غالْيَة ɣalya	غالْيِين ɣalyiin	أغْلَى ʔaɣla
good	كوِيِّس kuwayyis	كوِيِّسَة kuwayyisa	كوِيِّسِين kuwayyisiin	أحْسَن ʔaħsan
bad	وِحِش wiħiʃ	وِحْشَة wiħʃa	وِحْشِين wiħʃiin	أوْحَش ʔawħaʃ
thin	رُفَيَّع rufayyaʒ	رُفَيَّعَة rufayyaʒa	رُفَيَّعِين rufayyaʒiin	أرْفَع ʔarfaʒ
short	قُصَيَّر ʔuṣayyar	قُصَيَّرَة ʔuṣayyara	قُصَيَّرِين ʔuṣayyariin	أقْصَر ʔaʔṣar
difficult	صَعْب ṣaʒb	صَعْبَة ṣaʒba	صَعْبِين ṣaʒbiin	أصْعَب ʔaṣʒab

easy	سَهْل sahl	سَهْلَة sahla	سَهْلِين sahliin	أَسْهَل ʔashal
light (weight)	خَفِيف xafiif	خَفِيفَة xafiifa	خُفاف xufaaf	أَخَفّ ʔaxaff
heavy	تِقِيل tiʔiil	تِقِيلَة tiʔiila	تُقال tuʔaal	أَتْقَل ʔatʔal
old (human) / big	كِبِير kibiir	كِبِيرَة kibiira	كُبار kubaar	أَكْبَر ʔakbar
many	كِتِير kitiir	كِتِيرَة kitiira	كُتار kutaar	أَكْتَر ʔaktar
far	بِعِيد biʒiid	بِعِيدَة biʒiida	بُعاد buʒaad	أَبْعَد ʔabʒad
pleasant / delicious	لَذِيذ laziiz	لَذِيذَة laziiza	لُذاذ luzaaz	أَلَذّ ʔalazz
beautiful	جَمِيل gamiil	جَمِيلَة gamiila	جُمال gumaal	أَجْمَل ʔagmal

cheap	رِخِيص rixiiş	رِخِيصَة rixiişa	رُخاص ruxaaş	أرْخَص ʔarxaş
fat	تِخِين tixiin	تِخِينَة tixiina	تُخان tuxaan	أتْخَن ʔatxan
tall / long	طَوِيل ʧawiil	طَوِيلَة ʧawiila	طُوال ʧuwaal	أطْوَل ʔaʧwal
quick	سَرِيع sariiʒ	سَرِيعَة sariiʒa	سُراع suraaʒ	أسْرَع ʔasraʒ
slow	بَطِيء baʧʃiiʔ	بَطِيئَة baʧʃiiʔa	بُطاء buʧʃaaʔ	أبْطَأ ʔabʧʃaʔ
new	جِدِيد gidiid	جِدِيدَة gidiida	جُداد gudaad	أجْدَد ʔagdad
old (non-human)	قَدِيم ʔadiim	قَدِيمَة ʔadiima	قُدام ʔudaam	أقْدَم ʔaʔdam
clean	نِضِيف niḍiif	نِضِيفَة niḍiifa	نُضاف nuḍaaf	أنْضَف ʔanḍaf

intelligent	ذَكى zaki	ذَكِيَّة zakiyya	أَذْكِيا ʔazkiya	أَذْكى ʔazka
stupid	غَبِي ɣabi	غَبِيَّة ɣabiyya	أَغْبِيا ʔaɣbiya	أَغْبَى ʔaɣba
rich	غَنِي ɣani	غَنِيَّة ɣaniyya	أَغْنِيا ʔaɣniya	أَغْنَى ʔaɣna
poor	فَقِير faʔiir	فَقِيرَة faʔiira	فُقَرا fuʔara	أَفْقَر ʔafʔar

☾ Comparative and Superlative Statements

To form a comparison between two persons or things, use the comparative (المقارنة) form followed by the preposition مِن *(min)*. When comparing more than two persons or things, use the superlative (التفضيل) form followed by an indefinite noun.

Read through the following examples.

الـوَلَد ذَكِي والـبِنْت كَمـان ذَكِيَّة لَكِن الـوَلَد أَذْكى مِن الـبِنْت. هُوَّ أَذْكى وَلَد فـي الـفَصْل.
ilwalad zaki wi-ilbint kamaan zakiyya laakin ilwalad ʔazka min-ilbint. huwwa ʔazka walad fi-ilfaṣl.
The boy is intelligent. The girl is also intelligent. But the boy is more intelligent than the girl. He is the most intelligent boy in the class.

الـبَنـات طُـوال والأولاد كمـان طُـوال لكـن الـبنـات أطْـوَل مـن الأولاد. هُمَّ أطْـوَل بَنـات.	

ilbanaat ʃuwɑɑl wi-il?awlaad kamaan ʃuwɑɑl laakin ilbanaat ?atʃwɑl min-il?awlaad humma. ?atʃwɑl banaat.

The girls are tall. The boys are also tall. But the girls are taller than the boys. They are the tallest girls.

Participles Functioning as Adjectives

Participles that function as adjectives do not have comparative or superlative forms. An explanation of the active participle is provided in lesson 25. Here are some examples.

English Translation	Masculine Adjective	Feminine Adjective	Dual / Plural Adjectives
tired	تَعْبـان taʒbaan	تَعْبـانَـة taʒbaana	تَعْبـانيـن taʒbaniin
sick	عَيَّـان ʒayyaan	عَيَّانَـة ʒayyaana	عَيَّـانيـن ʒayyaniin
happy	فرْحـان farħaan	فرْحـانَـة farħaana	فرْحـانـيـن farħaniin
happy	مَبْسُوط mabsuuʈ	مَبْسُوطَـة mabsuuʈa	مَبْسُوطيـن mabsuʈiin
upset	زَعْلان zaʒlaan	زَعْلانَـة zaʒlaana	زَعْلانيـن zaʒlaniin
angry	مِتْنَرْفِز mitnarfiz	مِتْنَرْفِزَة mitnarfiza	مِتْنَرْفِزيـن mitnarfiziin
short-tempered	عَصَبـي ʒaṣabi	عَصَبـيَّـة ʒaṣabiyya	عَصَبـيَّيـن ʒaṣabiyyiin
worried	قَلْقـان ?al?aan	قَلْقـانَـة ?al?aana	قَلْقـانيـن ?al?aniin

fed-up, bored	زَهْقان zah?aan	زَهْقانَة zah?aana	زَهْقانِين zah?aniin
busy	مَشْغُول maʃɣuul	مَشْغُولَة maʃɣuula	مَشْغُولِين maʃɣuliin
free / empty	فاضِي faaḍi	فاضْيَة faḍya	فاضْيِين faḍyiin
present	مَوْجُود mawguud	مَوْجُودَة mawguuda	مَوْجُودِين mawgudiin
cold	بَرْدان bardaan	بَرْدانَة bardaana	بَرْدانِين bardaniin
hot	حَرّان ħarraan	حَرّانَة ħarraana	حَرّانِين ħarraniin
warm	دَفْيان dafyaan	دَفْيانَة dafyaana	دَفْيانِين dafyaaniin
hungry	جَعان gaʒaan	جَعانَة gaʒaana	جَعانِين gaʒaniin
full (opposite of hungry)	شَبْعان ʃabʒaan	شَبْعانَة ʃabʒaana	شَبْعانِين ʃabʒaniin
thirsty	عَطْشان ʒaʈʃaan	عَطْشانَة ʒaʈʃaana	عَطْشانِين ʒaʈʃaniin
in a hurry	مِسْتَعْجِل mistaʒgil	مِسْتَعْجِلَة mistaʒgila	مِسْتَعْجِلِين mistaʒgiliin
late	مِتْأَخَّر mit?axxar	مِتْأَخَّرَة mit?axxara	مِتْأَخَّرِين mit?axxariin

Agreement

Adjectives should agree with the nouns they describe in gender, number, and whether or not they are definite.

◟ Gender
A masculine singular noun should be followed by a masculine singular adjective.

وَلَد لَطِيف	walad laṭṭiif	a nice boy

A feminine singular noun should be followed by a feminine singular adjective.

بِنْت لَطِيفَة	bint laṭṭiifa	a nice girl

◟ Number
Dual nouns (masculine or feminine) and plural human nouns (masculine or feminine) are followed by plural adjectives.

وَلَدِين لُطاف	waladeen luṭṭaaf	two nice boys
بِنْتِين لُطاف	binteen luṭṭaaf	two nice girls
أَوْلاد لُطاف	ʔawlaad luṭṭaaf	nice boys / children
بَنات لُطاف	banaat luṭṭaaf	nice girls

Plural non-human nouns are followed by feminine singular adjectives.

كُتُب جِدِيدَة	kutub gidiida	new books

◟ The definite article
The noun and adjective should both be either definite or indefinite in an adjectival phrase (noun–adjective).

البِنْت الطَّوِيلَة وَرا البِيت.	ilbint-iṭṭawiila wara-ilbeet
The <u>tall girl</u> is behind the house.	
ورا البِيت بِنْت طَوِيلَة.	wara-ilbeet bint- ṭawiila
Behind the house there is <u>a tall girl</u>.	

If the adjective functions as the predicate in a nominal sentence, rather than as part of the adjectival phrase, the adjective should always remain indefinite.

البِنْت لَطيفة.	ilbint laṭiifa
The girl is nice.	

Exercise 1
Choose the correct word for each sentence.

Example:

السُّوبَر مـارْكِت (قُرَيِّب – قُرَيِّبَة – قُرَيِّبِين).

١- الشُّقَق دِي (جِدِيد – جِدِيدَة – جُداد).

٢- الدَّرْسِين دُول (صَعْب – صَعْبَة – صَعْبِين).

٣- قَرايِب بـابـاه (غَنِي – غَنِيَّة – أغْنِيا).

٤- بِيت جِدّي (واسِع – واسْعَـة – واسْعِـين).

٥- الفُسْتـان دا (غـالِي – غـالْيَة – غـالْيِين).

٦- مُوَظَّف البَنْك مِش (تَعْبـان – تَعْبـانَة – تَعْبـانِين).

٧- عَرَبِيِّتْها (سَريع – سَريعَة – سُراع).

٨- السّـاعَـة والنَّضّـارَة (رِخيص – رِخيصَة – رُخـاص).

٩- خـالْتُـه مِش (فَقِير – فَقِيرَة – فُقَرا).

١٠-جِدّي وجِدّتِي (عَصَبِي – عَصَبِيَّة – عَصَبِيِّين).

Exercise 2

Complete each sentence by forming a comparative adjective from the word provided.

Example:

الْعَرَبِيَّة ـــــــــــــــــ الأُتُوبِيس. (صُغَيَّر)
الْعَرَبِيَّة **أَصْغَر مِن** الأُتُوبِيس.

١ـ الْبُرْتُقانَة ـــــــــــــــــ التُّفَّاحَة. (كِبِير)

٢ـ الرَّاجِل ـــــــــــــــــ السِّتّ. (تِخِين)

٣ـ الطِّفْل دا ـــــــــــــــــ الطِّفْل دا. (فَقِير)

٤ـ الْهُدُوم الْمُسْتَوْرَدَة ـــــــــــــــــ الْهُدُوم دِي. (غَالِي)

٥ـ الشَّقَّة بِتاعْتِي ـــــــــــــــــ شَقَّةْ جِدِّي. (ضَيَّق)

٦ـ جامْعِةُ الْقاهِرَة ـــــــــــــــــ الْجامْعَة الأَمْرِيكِيَّة. (قَدِيم)

٧ـ هَرَم خُوفُو ـــــــــــــــــ هَرَم مَنْقَرَع. (طَوِيل)

٨ـ الْقَطْر ـــــــــــــــــ الْعَرَبِيَّة. (سَرِيع)

٩ـ يُوسِف ـــــــــــــــــ أَخُوه. (ذَكِي)

١٠ـ شُغْلَها ـــــــــــــــــ بِيتْها. (بِعِيد)

Exercise 3

Complete each sentence by selecting the adjective with the opposite meaning to the one in the sentence.

Example:

الشَّقَّة كِبيرة. المَكْتَب _____ .

وِحِش – جِديد – واسِع – <u>صُغَيَّر</u> – قَديم

١- البِيت جِديد. الشَّقَّة _____ .

بَرْدانَة – بَطِيئَة – ضَيِّقَة – قَديمَة – وِحْشَة

٢- لَيْلى طَويلَة. يُوسِف _____ .

مَبْسُوط – جَعان – رُفَيَّع – قُصَيَّر – كِبير

٣- المَكْتَب واسِع. الشَّوارِع _____ .

ضَيِّقَة – بَرْدانَة – وِحْشَة – قَديمَة – بَطِيئَة

٤- أنا شَبْعان. أصْحابي _____ .

رُفَيَّعِين – كُبار – قُصَيَّرِين – جَعانِين – مَبْسُوطِين

٥- سَلْوَى تِخينَة. أخُوها _____ .

كِبير – قُصَيَّر – رُفَيَّع – جَعان – مَبْسُوط

٦- إحْنا حَرّانِين. هِيَّ _____ .

بَرْدانَة – قَديمَة – وِحْشَة – ضَيِّقَة – بَطِيئَة

٧- العَرَبِيَّة سَريعَة. الأُتُوبِيس _____ .

ضَيِّق – كِبير – قَديم – بَطِيء – وِحِش

٨- إنْتِي زَعْلانَة. إحْنا _____ .

قُصَيَّرِين – رُفَيَّعِين – كُبار – مَبْسُوطِين – جَعانِين

٩- الأطْفال حِلْوِين. البِنْت _____ .

ضَيِّقَة – بَرْدانَة – بَطِيئَة – قَديمَة – وِحْشَة

١٠- مامْتُه صُغَيَّرَة. باباه _____ .

جَعان – قُصَيَّر – رُفَيَّع – كِبير – مَبْسُوط

Exercise 4

For each noun, choose the adjective that could not describe it.

Example:

بِيتْها (واسِع – جِديد – ـ<u>تِخِين</u> – رِخِيص)

١ـ الْجَامْعَة (غَالْيَة – جَعانَة – كُوَيِّسَة – بِعيدَة).

٢ـ اِبْنَها (لَطِيف – رُفَيَّع – رِخِيص – ذَكِي).

٣ـ أساتْذِةُ أُخْتِي (لُطاف – أغْنِيا – قُدام – طُوال).

٤ـ الدُّرُوس (شَبْعانَة – طَويلَة – سَهْلَة – جِديدَة).

٥ـ شَقَّتْهُم (كِبِيرَة – واسْعَة – نِضِيفَة – بَردانَة).

٦ـ أصْحابِي (بُطاء – تُخان – واسْعِين – تَعْبانِين).

٧ـ بِيتُه (مَشْغُول – رِخِيص – قُرِيّب – قَدِيم).

٨ـ الْقِصَّة (صَعْبَة – قُصَيَّرَة – تِخِينَة – كُوَيِّسَة).

٩ـ الْقَمِيص (ضَيَّق – غالِي – نِضِيف – فاضِي).

١٠ـ عَرَبِيتِي (جِديدَة – واطْيَة – غالْيَة – كِبِيرَة).

Example:

‫- الْفِيلْم دا قَدِيم.‬ (This film is old.)
‫دا أَقْدَم فِيلْم.‬ (This is the oldest film.)

‫١- الْمُفْرَدات دِي سَهْلَة.‬

_____

‫٢- الجـامْعَة دِي قُرَيّبَة.‬

_____

‫٣- الرّاجِل دا فَقِير.‬

_____

‫٤- الطُّلّاب دُول أَذْكِيا.‬

_____

‫٥- الجَّزْمَة دِي ضَيِّقَة.‬

_____

‫٦- الْعُمارَة دِي عالْيَة.‬

_____

‫٧- الأتُوبِيس دا سَرِيع.‬

_____

‫٨- الْقَلَم دا رِخِيص.‬

_____

‫٩- البَنـات دُول جُمـال.‬

_____

‫١٠- الشَّنْطَة دِي حِلْوَة.‬

_____

Lesson 12: Numbers

How to Read and Pronounce Numbers (الأعداد والأرقام)

Number	Transliterated Form	Number	Transliterated Form
صِفْر / زِيرُو 0	ziiru / şifr	حِداشَر 11	ħidaaʃar
واحِد 1	waaħid	إِثْـنـاشَر 12	itnaaʃar
إِثْنِين 2	itneen	تَلَتَّـاشَر 13	talattaaʃar
ثَلاثَة 3	talaata	أَرْبَعْتـاشَر 14	ʔarbaʒtaaʃar
أَرْبَعَة 4	ʔarbaʒa	خَمَسْتـاشَر 15	xamastaaʃar
خَمْسَة 5	xamsa	سِتَّـاشَر 16	sittaaʃar
سِتَّة 6	sitta	سَبَعْتـاشَر 17	sabaʒtaaʃar
سَبْعَة 7	sabʒa	تَمَنْتـاشَر 18	tamantaaʃar
تَمَانْيَة 8	tamanya	تِسَعْتـاشَر 19	tisaʒtaaʃar
تِسْعَة 9	tisʒa	عِشْرِين 20	ʒiʃriin
عَشَرَة 10	ʒaʃara		

تَلاتِين	talatiin	مِيتِين	miteen
30		200	
إرْبِعِين	?irbiʒiin	تُلْتُمِيَّة	tultumiyya
40		300	
خَمْسِين	xamsiin	رُبْعُمِيَّة	rubʒumiyya
50		400	
سِتِّين	sittiin	خُمْسُمِيَّة	xumsumiyya
60		500	
سَبْعِين	sabʒiin	سُتُّمِيَّة	suttumiyya
70		600	
تَمانِين	tamaniin	سُبْعُمِيَّة	subʒumiyya
80		700	
تِسْعِين	tisʒiin	تُمْنُمِيَّة	tumnumiyya
90		800	
مِيَّة	miyya	تُسْعُمِيَّة	tusʒumiyya
100		900	
		أَلْف	?alf
		1,000	

أَلْفِين 2,000	ʔalfeen	سَبَع آلاف 7,000	sabaʒtalaaf
تَلَت آلاف 3,000	talattalaaf	تَمَن آلاف 8,000	tamantalaaf
أَرْبَع آلاف 4,000	ʔarbaʒtalaaf	تِسَع آلاف 9,000	tisaʒtalaaf
خَمَس آلاف 5,000	xamastalaaf	عَشْر آلاف 10,000	ʒaʃartalaaf
سِتّ آلاف 6,000	sittalaaf		

To read and pronounce numbers 21 through 99, begin with the right-hand digit, add و (transliteration: *wi*; meaning: and), and then the left-hand digit.

واحِد وعِشْرِين	waaħid wi-ʒiʃriin	21

From 100 to 120, begin with 100, insert the word و, and then add the number from 1 through 20.

مِيَّة وواحِد	miyya wi-waaħid	101

From 121 to 999, begin with 100 (or its multiples), then add the number from 21 through 99.

مِيَّة واحِد وعِشْرِين	miyya waaħid wi-ʒiʃriin	121
مِيَّة سِتَّة وخَمْسِين	miyya sitta wi-xamsiin	156
رُبْعُمِيَّة وسِتَّاشَر	rubʒumiyya w-sittaaʃar	416

Starting from 11,000, pronounce the number of thousands first
and then the word ألف (transliateration: *?alf;* meaning: a thousand).

حـداشَـر ألـف	ħidaaʃar ?alf	11,000

How to Use Numbers
⤷ Number 1
To refer to 1 of something, use the object in its singular, indefinite
form without the word for 1. To add emphasis, put the number 1 after
the object.

عـايِز كِـتـاب.	ʒaayiz ketaab	I want a book.
عـايِز كِـتـاب واجِـد.	ʒaayiz ketaab waaħid	I want just one book.

⤷ Number 2
To refer to 2 of something, use the dual form of the noun without the
word for 2. The dual is formed by adding the suffix يـن *(een)* to the
singular noun.

كِـتـاب	ketaab	book
كِـتـابِـيـن	ketabeen	two books

⤷ Numbers 3–10
The numbers 3 through 10 should be followed by plural nouns.
When followed by a noun, any long middle vowels in the number
are shortened and the final feminine marker ـة / ة *(ta marbuuʈa)* is
dropped.

تـلاتـة ← تـلـت	talaata → talat
تـلَـت كُـتُـب	talat kutub (three books)

▥ Exceptions
When numbers are used to order food or drink or to quantify weight
or money, then singular nouns follow the number.

In these cases, where the numbers 3 through 10 are followed by singular nouns, a long middle vowel remains as it is and/or the final ـة / ة *(ta marbuuťa)* is not dropped.

ثَلاثَة سَلَطَة	talaata salaťa	three salads (literally: three salad)
أرْبَعَة عَصِـير	ʔarbaʒa ʒaṣiir	four juices (literally: four juice)
خَمْسَة كِيلُو	xamsa kiilu	five kilos (literally: five kilo)
عَشْرَة جِنِيه	ʒaʃara gineeh	ten pounds (literally: ten pound)

ᗌ **Numbers great than 10**
Numbers greater than 10 are always followed by singular nouns.

جِداشَر كِتاب	ħidaaʃar ketaab	eleven books (literally: eleven book)
مِيت كتاب	miit ketaab	one hundred books (literally: one hundred book)

Exercise 1
Choose the correct translation for each sentence.

Example:
These are twenty pens.

- فِيـه عِشْرِيـن قَلَـم.
- <u>دُول عِشْرِيـن قَلَـم.</u>
- مَفِيـش عِشْرِيـن قَلَـم.

1. These are twelve dictionaries.

- فِيـه اتـنـاشَـر قـامُـوس.
- مَفِيـش اتنـاشَـر قـامُـوس.
- دول اثْنـاشَر قـامُـوس.

2. There are seven books on the desk.

- دول سبـع كُتُب عَلى المكتب.
- فِيـه سبـع كُتُب عَلى المكتب.
- مَفِيـش سبـع كُتُب عَلى المكتب.

3. These are five teachers.

- دول خمـس مـدرِّسِـين.
- فِيـه خمـس مـدرِّسِـين.
- مَفِيـش خمـس مـدرِّسِـين.

4. In the classroom, there are 63 students.

- فِي الـفـصـل تـلاتـة وستِّيـن طـالِـب.
- فِي الـفـصـل مَفِيـش تـلاتـة وستِّيـن طـالِـب.
- فِي الـفـصـل دول تـلاتـة وستِّيـن طـالِـب.

5. These are ninety-six pens.

- دول ستَّة وتسـعِيـن قلـم.
- فِيـه ستَّة وتسـعِيـن قلـم.
- مَفِيـش ستَّة وتسـعِيـن قلـم.

6. On this street, there are fourteen houses.

- فِي الشَّارِع دا دُول أَرْبَعْتَاشَر بِيت.
- فِي الشّارِع دا أربعتاشَر بِيت.
- فِي الشّارِع دا مَفِيش أربعتاشَر بِيت.

7. In the apartment, there are two bathrooms.

- فِي الشّقة دُول حمَّامِين.
- فِي الشّقة حمَّامِين.
- فِي الشّقة مَفِيش حمَّامِين.

8. These are forty-eight shirts.

- فِيه تمانْيـة وإربِعِين قمِيص.
- مَفِيش تمانْيـة وإربِعِين قمِيص.
- دول تمانْيـة وإربِعِين قمِيص.

9. There are four buses in the university.

- دول أرْبَع أتُوبِيسات فِي الجامْعة.
- فِيه أرْبَع أتُوبِيسات فِي الجامْعة.
- مَفِيش أرْبَع أتُوبِيسات فِي الجامْعة.

10. There are not nine books here.

- دول تِسع كُتُب هنا.
- فِيه تِسع كُتُب هنا.
- مَفِيش تِسع كُتُب هنا.

Exercise 2
Imagine you are in a restaurant, supermarket, or bookstore and try to order five items using the numbers you have learned.

Lesson 13: Telling the Time

The following table shows how to tell the time (الوقت / الزمن), using examples between 1 o'clock and 2 o'clock which can be applied to all other times of day.

Time	Transliterated Form	English Translation
السَّاعَـة واحْدَة (بـالظَّـبْط).	issaaʒa waħda (bizzˤabtˤ)	It is 1 o'clock (exactly).
السَّـاعَـة واحْدَة ودِقِيـقَـة.	issaaʒa waħda wi-dʔiiʔa	It is 1:01. (literally: it is one and a minute.)
السَّـاعَـة واحْدَة ودِقيقْـتِـيـن.	issaaʒa waħda wi-dʔiʔteen	It is 1:02. (literally: it is one and two minutes.)
السَّـاعَـة واحْدَة وتَلَـت دَقـايِـق.	issaaʒa waħda wi-talat daʔaayiʔ	It is 1:03. (literally: it is one and three minutes.)
السَّـاعَـة واحْدَة وأرْبَـع دَقـايِـق.	issaaʒa waħda w-ʔarbaʒ daʔaayiʔ	It is 1:04. (literally: it is one and four minutes.)
السَّـاعَـة واحْدَة وخَـمْسَـة.	issaaʒa waħda wi-xamsa	It is 1:05. (literally: it is one and five.)
السَّـاعَـة واحْدَة وسِتّ دَقـايِـق.	issaaʒa waħda wi-sitti-daʔaayiʔ	It is 1:06. (literally: it is one and six minutes.)
السَّـاعَـة واحْدَة وسَبَـع دَقـايِـق.	issaaʒa waħda wi-sabaʒ daʔaayiʔ	It is 1:07. (literally: it is one and seven minutes.)
السَّـاعَـة واحْدَة وتَمَـن دَقـايِـق.	issaaʒa waħda wi-taman daʔaayiʔ	It is 1:08. (literally: it is one and eight minutes.)
السَّـاعَـة واحْدَة وتِسَـع دَقـايِـق.	issaaʒa waħda wi-tisaʒ daʔaayiʔ	It is 1:09. (literally: it is one and nine minutes.)

السَّـاعَـة واحْـدَة وِعَـشْـرَة.	issaaʒa waħda wi-ʒaʃara	It is 1:10. (literally: it is one and ten.)
السَّـاعَـة واحْـدَة وِحْداشَـر دِقِـيـقَـة.	issaaʒa waħda wi-ħdaaʃar diʔiiʔa	It is 1:11. (literally: it is one and eleven minutes.)
السَّـاعَـة واحْـدَة وِاثْنـاشَـر دِقِـيـقَـة.	issaaʒa waħda w-itnaaʃar diʔiiʔa	It is 1:12. (literally: it is one and twelve minutes.)
السَّـاعَـة واحْـدَة وِتَّلَتّـاشَـر دِقِـيـقَـة.	issaaʒa waħda wi-talattaaʃar diʔiiʔa	It is 1:13. (literally: it is one and thirteen minutes.)
السَّـاعَـة واحْـدَة وْأَرْبَـعْتـاشَـر دِقِـيـقَـة.	issaaʒa waħda w-ʔarbaʒtaaʃar diʔiiʔa	It is 1:14. (literally: it is one and fourteen minutes.)
السَّـاعَـة واحْـدَة وْرُبْع.	issaaʒa waħda w-rubʒ	It is 1:15. (literally: it is one and a quarter.)
السَّـاعَـة واحْـدَة وِسِتّـاشَـر دِقِـيـقَـة.	issaaʒa waħda wi-sittaaʃar diʔiiʔa	It is 1:16. (literally: it is one and sixteen minutes.)
السَّـاعَـة واحْـدَة وِسَبَـعْتـاشَـر دِقِـيـقَـة.	issaaʒa waħda wi-sabaʒtaaʃar diʔiiʔa	It is 1:17. (literally: it is one and seventeen minutes.)
السَّـاعَـة واحْـدَة وِتَـمَنْتـاشَـر دِقِـيـقَـة.	issaaʒa waħda wi-tamantaaʃar diʔiiʔa	It is 1:18. (literally: it is one and eighteen minutes.)
السَّـاعَـة واحْـدَة وِتِسَـعْتـاشَـر دِقِـيـقَـة.	issaaʒa waħda wi-tisaʒtaaʃar diʔiiʔa	It is 1:19. (literally: it is one and nineteen minutes.)
السَّـاعَـة واحْـدَة وْتِلْت.	issaaʒa waħda w-tilt	It is 1:20. (literally: it is one and a third.)

السَّاعَة واحْدَة وْتِلْت وِدْقِيقَة.	issaaʒa waħda w-tilt wi-dʔiiʔa	It is 1:21. (literally: it is one and a third and a minute.)
السَّاعَة واحْدَة وْتِلْت وِدْقِيقْتِين.	issaaʒa waħda w-tilt wi-dʔiʔteen	It is 1:22. (literally: it is one and a third and two minutes.)
السَّاعَة واحْدَة وْتِلْت وْتَلَت دَقايِق.	issaaʒa waħda w-tilt wi-talat daʔaayiʔ	It is 1:23. (literally: it is one and a third and three minutes.)
السَّاعَة واحْدَة وْتِلْت وأرْبَع دَقايِق.	issaaʒa waħda w-tilt w-ʔarbaʒ daʔaayiʔ	It is 1:24. (literally: it is one and a third and four minutes.)
السَّاعَة واحْدَة وْنُصّ إلّا خَمْسَة.	issaaʒa waħda w-nuṣṣ-illa xamsa	It is 1:25. (literally: it is one and a half minus five.)
السَّاعَة واحْدَة وْنُصّ إلّا أرْبَع دَقايِق.	issaaʒa waħda w-nuṣṣ-illa-rbaʒ daʔaayiʔ	It is 1:26. (literally: it is one and a half minus four minutes.)
السَّاعَة واحْدَة وْنُصّ إلّا تَلَت دَقايِق.	issaaʒa waħda w-nuṣṣ-illa talat daʔaayiʔ	It is 1:27. (literally: it is one and a half minus three minutes.)
السَّاعَة واحْدَة وْنُصّ إلّا دْقِيقْتِين.	issaaʒa waħda w-nuṣṣ-illa-dʔiʔteen	It is 1:28. (literally: it is one and a half minus two minutes.)
السَّاعَة واحْدَة وْنُصّ إلّا دْقِيقَة.	issaaʒa waħda w-nuṣṣ-illa-dʔiiʔa	It is 1:29. (literally: it is one and a half minus a minute.)

السَّاعَـة واحْدَة وْنُـصّ.	issaaʒa waħda w-nuṣṣ	It is 1:30. (literally: it is one and a half.)
السَّاعَـة واحْدَة وْنُـصّ وِدْقيقَـة.	issaaʒa waħda w-nuṣṣ wi-dʔiiʔa	It is 1:31. (literally: it is one and a half plus a minute.)
السَّاعَـة واحْدَة وْنُـصّ وِدْقيـقْتِـين.	issaaʒa waħda w-nuṣṣ wi-dʔiʔteen	It is 1:32. (literally: it is one and a half plus two minutes.)
السَّاعَـة واحْدَة وْنُـصّ وِتَـلَت دَقـايِق.	issaaʒa waħda w-nuṣṣ wi-talat daʔaayiʔ	It is 1:33. (literally: it is one and a half plus three minutes.)
السَّاعَـة واحْدَة وْنُـصّ وأرْبَـع دَقـايِق.	issaaʒa waħda w-nuṣṣ w-ʔarbaʒ daʔaayiʔ	It is 1:34. (literally: it is one and a half plus four minutes.)
السَّاعَـة واحْدَة وْنُـصّ وْخَـمْسَـة.	issaaʒa waħda w-nuṣṣ w-xamsa	It is 1:35. (literally: it is one and a half plus five.)
السَّاعَـة واحْدَة وْنُـصّ وِستّ دَقـايِق.	issaaʒa waħda w-nuṣṣ wi-sitti-daʔaayiʔ	It is 1:36. (literally: it is one and a half plus six minutes.)
السَّاعَـة واحْدَة وْنُـصّ وِسَـبَع دَقـايِق.	issaaʒa waħda w-nuṣṣ wi-sabaʒ daʔaayiʔ	It is 1:37. (literally: it is one and a half plus seven minutes.)
السَّاعَـة واحْدَة وْنُـصّ وِتَـمَن دَقـايِق.	issaaʒa waħda w-nuṣṣ wi-taman daʔaayiʔ	It is 1:38. (literally: it is one and a half plus eight minutes.)

السَّـاعَـة واحْـدَة وْنُـصّ وِتِسَـع دَقـايِـق.	issaaʒa waħda w-nuṣṣ wi-tisaʒ daʔaayiʔ	It is 1:39. (literally: it is one and a half plus nine minutes.)
السَّـاعَـة اِتْنِـين إلّا تِلْـت.	issaaʒa itneen-illa tilt	It is 1:40. (literally: it is two minus a third.)
السَّـاعـة اِتْنِـين إلّا تِسـعْتـاشَر دِقيقـة.	issaaʒa itneen-illa tisaʒtaaʃar diʔiiʔa	It is 1:41. (literally: it is two minus nineteen minutes.)
السَّـاعَـة اِتْنِـين إلّا تَمَنْتـاشَر دِقيقَـة.	issaaʒa itneen-illa tamantaaʃar diʔiiʔa	It is 1:42. (literally: it is two minus eighteen minutes.)
السَّـاعـة اتنِـين إلّا سبـعتـاشَر دقيقـة.	issaaʒa itneen-illa sabaʒtaaʃar diʔiiʔa	It is 1:43. (literally: it is two minus seventeen minutes.)
السَّـاعَـة اِتْنِـين إلّا سِتّـاشَر دِقيقَـة.	issaaʒa itneen-illa sittaaʃar diʔiiʔa	It is 1:44. (literally: it is two minus sixteen minutes.)
السَّـاعَـة اِتْنِـين إلّا رُبْع.	issaaʒa itneen-illa rubʒ	It is 1:45. (literally: it is two minus a quarter.)
السَّـاعـة اتنِـين إلّا أربـعتـاشـر دِقيقـة.	issaaʒa itneen-illa ʔarbaʒtaaʃar diʔiiʔa	It is 1:46. (literally: it is two minus fourteen minutes.)
السَّـاعَـة اِتْنِـين إلّا تَلَتّـاشَر دِقيقَـة.	issaaʒa itneen-illa talattaaʃar diʔiiʔa	It is 1:47. (literally: it is two minus thirteen minutes.)

السَّاعَة اِثْنِين إِلّا اِتْنـاشَر دِقِيـقَة.	issaaʒa itneen-illa itnaaʃar diʔiiʔa	It is 1:48. (literally: it is two minus twelve minutes.)
السَّاعَة اِثْنِين إِلّا حِداشَر دِقِيـقَّة.	issaaʒa itneen-illa ħidaaʃar diʔiiʔa	It is 1:49. (literally: it is two minus eleven minutes.)
السَّاعَة اِثْنِين إِلّا عَشَرَة.	issaaʒa itneen-illa ʒaʃara	It is 1:50. (literally: it is two minus ten.)
السَّاعَة اِثْنِين إِلّا تِسَع دَقايِق.	issaaʒa itneen-illa tisaʒ daʔaayiʔ	It is 1:51. (literally: it is two minus nine minutes.)
السَّاعَة اِثْنِين إِلّا تَمَن دَقايِق.	issaaʒa itneen-illa taman daʔaayiʔ	It is 1:52. (literally: it is two minus eight minutes.)
السَّاعَة اِثْنِين إِلّا سَبَع دَقايِق.	issaaʒa itneen-illa sabaʒ daʔaayiʔ	It is 1:53. (literally: it is two minus seven minutes.)
السَّاعَة اِثْنِين إِلّا سِتّ دَقايِق.	issaaʒa itneen-illa sitti-daʔaayiʔ	It is 1:54. (literally: it is two minus six minutes.)
السَّاعَة اِثْنِين إِلّا خَمْسَة.	issaaʒa itneen-illa xamsa	It is 1:55. (literally: it is two minus five.)
السَّاعَة اِثْنِين إِلّا أرْبَع دَقايِق.	issaaʒa itneen-illa ʔarbaʒ daʔaayiʔ	It is 1:56. (literally: it is two minus four minutes.)
السَّاعَة اِثْنِين إِلّا تَلَت دَقايِق.	issaaʒa itneen-illa talat daʔaayiʔ	It is 1:57. (literally: it is two minus three minutes.)
السَّاعَة اِثْنِين إِلّا دُقِيقْتِين.	issaaʒa itneen-illa dʔiʔteen	It is 1:58. (literally: it is two minus two minutes.)

السَّاعَة اِثْنِين إلّا دْقِيقَة.	issaaʒa itneen-illa dʔiiʔa	It is 1:59. (literally: it is two minus a minute.)
السَّاعَة اِثْنِين (بِالظَّبْط).	issaaʒa itneen (bizzabtʃ)	It is 2 o'clock (exactly).

Exercise 1

In the following paragraph, rewrite the times given in numerals using words from the box below.

> جداشَر إلا رُبْع – سبعة وعشرة – اِثْناشَر ونُصّ وخَمْسَة – تسعة – تلاتة – تسعة وخمسة – سِتَّة وعشرة – سبعة ونُصّ – جِداشَر ونُصّ وخَمْسَة – تمانْيَة – تمانْيَة إلّا تِلْت – اِثْنِين – تمانية وتِلْت

أنا دلوقتِي فِي البيت والسَّاعَة ٧:٣٠ ـــــــــــــــــــــــــ .

الأخبـار فِي الـرادْيُو الساعَة ٧:٤٠ ـــــــــــــــــــــــــ .

أتوبيس الجامْعة الساعَة ٨:٢٠ ـــــــــــــــــــــــــ .

فصـل الـعرَبِي الساعَة ٩:٠٥ ـــــــــــــــــــــــــ وفصـل الـتـاريـخ

الساعَة ١٠:٤٥ ـــــــــــــــــــــــــ وفصـل الـعُلُـوم السِّيـاسِيَّة

الساعَة ١٢:٣٥ ـــــــــــــــــــــــــ .

الـغدا فِي الـكـافِيتِيريـا الساعة ٢:٠٠ ـــــــــــــــــــــــــ الـدِّراسـة

فِي المكتَبَة الساعة ٣:٠٠ ـــــــــــــــــــــــــ .

تمرين الجيم الساعة ٧:١٠ ـــــــــــــــــــــــــ .

والـعشـا فِي البيت الساعة ٩:٠٠ ـــــــــــــــــــــــــ .

Exercise 2

Read aloud the times of Mr. Ashraf's activities in the timetable.

Shower	6:00 a.m.
Breakfast	6:15 a.m.
Coffee	6:40 a.m.
Radio news	6:50 a.m.
Bus	7:10 a.m.
Bank	7:35 a.m.
Landlord appointment	1:05 p.m.
Lunch	3:20 p.m.
Tea	6:15 p.m.
Gym	7:00 p.m.
Film	11:00 p.m.

Exercise 3

Using the template of Mr. Ashraf's timetable, create your own timetable for Friday.

Lesson 14: Conjugation of Past Tense Verbs

The root of the past tense verb (الفعل الماضي) is always refered to by the pronoun 'he,' to which we add suffixes to conjugate for the rest of the pronouns.

Verbs of Two Consonants

In verbs consisting of two consonants, the first consonant has a *fatħa* (short 'a').

For example, كَل (transliteration: *kal*; meaning: to eat).

Personal Pronoun	Past Tense Verb
هُوَّ huwwa he	كَل kal
هِيَّ heyya she	كَلِت kalit
هُمَّ humma they (d./p.)	كَلُوا kalu
إِنْتَ ʔenta you (m. s.)	كَلْت kalt
إِنْتِي ʔenti you (f. s.)	كَلْتِي kalti
إِنْتُو ʔentu you (d./p.)	كَلْتُوا kaltu
أَنَا ʔana I	كَلْت kalt

إِحْنـا	كَلْنـا
ʔeḥna	kalna
we	

Verbs of Three or More Consonants with *Fatha*

The following table shows the conjugation of verbs such as these:
- Verbs of three consonants with a *fatha* (short 'a') on the first and second consonants, for example, خَرَج (transliteration: *xarag*; meaning: to go out / leave);
- Verbs of more than three consonants with a *fatha* (short 'a') on the first or middle consonants, for example خَلَّص (transliteration: *xallaṣ*; meaning: to finish), إِثْكَلَّم (transliteration: *itkallim*; meaning: to talk / speak).

The appropriate past tense suffixes are then added to the verbs.

Personal Pronoun	خَرَج *xarag* to go out / leave	خَلَّص *xallaṣ* to finish	إِثْكَلَّم *itkallim* to talk / speak
هُوَّ huwwa he	خَرَج xarag	خَلَّص xallaṣ	إِثْكَلَّم itkallim
هِيَّ heyya she	خَرَجِت xaragit	خَلَّصِت xallaṣit	إِثْكَلَّمِت itkallimit
هُمَّ humma they (d./p.)	خَرَجُوا xaragu	خَلَّصُوا xallaṣu	إِثْكَلَّمُوا itkallimu
إِنْتَ ʔenta you (m. s.)	خَرَجْت xaragt	خَلَّصْت xallaṣt	إِثْكَلَّمْت itkallimt

إِنْتِي	خَرَجْتِي	خَلَّصْتِي	اِتْكَلِّمْتِي
?enti	xaragti	xallaṣti	itkallimti
you (f. s.)			
إِنْتُو	خَرَجْتُوا	خَلَّصْتُوا	اِتْكَلِّمْتُوا
?entu	xaragtu	xallaṣtu	itkallimtu
you (d./p.)			
أنا	خَرَجْت	خَلَّصْت	اِتْكَلِّمْت
?ana	xaragt	xallaṣt	itkallimt
I			
إِحْنا	خَرَجْنا	خَلَّصْنا	اِتْكَلِّمْنا
?eḥna	xaragna	xallaṣna	itkallimna
we			

Verbs with _Kasra_

The following table shows the conjugation of verbs such as these:

- Verbs consisting of three consonants with a _kasra_ (short 'i') on the first and second consonants, for example, شِرِب (transliteration: _ʃirib_; meaning: to drink);
- Verbs consisting of four letters, in which the second letter is ا (long 'aa') and the third letter has a _kasra_ (short 'i'), for example قابِل (transliteration: _?aabil;_ meaning: to meet).

For the pronouns هِيَّ (heyya) and هُمَّ (humma) drop the second _kasra_ (short 'i') before adding the appropriate past tense suffixes.

Personal Pronoun	شِرِب _ʃirib_ to drink	قابِل _?aabil_ to meet
هُوَّ huwwa he	شِرِب ʃirib	قابِل ?aabil

هِيَّ heyya she	شِرْبِت ʃirbit	قـابْلِت ʔablit
هُمَّ humma they (d./p.)	شِرْبُوا ʃirbu	قـابْلُوا ʔablu
إِنْتَ ʔenta you (m. s.)	شِرِبْت ʃiribt	قـابِلْت ʔabilt
إِنْتِي ʔenti you (f. s.)	شِرِبْتِي ʃiribti	قـابِلْتِي ʔabilti
إِنْتُو ʔentu you (d./p.)	شِرِبْتُوا ʃiribtu	قـابِلْتُوا ʔabiltu
أنـا ʔana I	شِرِبْت ʃiribt	قـابِلْت ʔabilt
إِحْنـا ʔeħna we	شِرِبْنـا ʃiribna	قـابِلْنـا ʔabilna

Verbs of Two Consonants with Second Consonant Doubled

In verbs with a *ʃadda* (doubling) on the second consonant, add the sound 'ee' (like the 'ai' in the English word 'straight') before adding the past tense suffixes. This applies to all pronouns except هِيَّ (heyya) and هُمَّ (humma).

For example, بصّ (transliteration: *baṣṣ;* meaning: to look).

Personal Pronoun	بَصّ *baṣṣ* to look
هُوَّ huwwa he	بَصّ baṣṣ
هِيَّ heyya she	بَصِّت baṣṣit
هُمَّ humma they (d./p.)	بَصُّوا baṣṣu
إنْتَ ʔenta you (m. s.)	بَصِّيت baṣṣeet
إنْتِي ʔenti you (f. s.)	بَصِّيتِي baṣṣeeti
إنْتُو ʔentu you (d./p.)	بَصِّيتُوا baṣṣeetu
أنا ʔana I	بَصِّيت baṣṣeet
إحْنـا ʔeħna we	بَصِّينـا baṣṣeena

Verbs Ending with ى (ʔalif maksuura)

In verbs ending with an ى (ʔalif maksuura, 'broken a'), drop the ى and add the sound 'ee' (as the 'ai' in the English word 'straight') before adding the past tense suffixes. This applies to all pronouns except هِيَّ (heyya) and هُمَّ (humma).

For example, اِسْتَنَّى (transliteration: istanna; meaning: to wait (for)).

Personal Pronoun	اِسْتَنَّى *istanna* to wait (for)
هُوَّ huwwa he	اِسْتَنَّى istanna
هِيَّ heyya she	اِسْتَنَّت istannit
هُمَّ humma they (d./p.)	اِسْتَنُّوا istannu
إِنْتَ ʔenta you (m. s.)	اِسْتَنَّيِت istanneet
إِنْتِي ʔenti you (f. s.)	اِسْتَنَّيِتِي istanneeti
إِنْتُو ʔentu you (d./p.)	اِسْتَنَّيِتُوا istanneetu

أَنـا	اِسْتَـنّـيـت
?ana	istanneet
I	

إِحْنـا	اِسْتَـنّـيـنـا
?eħna	istanneena
we	

Verbs Ending with ي (ya?)

In verbs ending with ي (ya?, long 'ii'), add the past tense suffixes as usual. This applies to all pronouns except هِيَّ (heyya) and هُمَّ (humma), where the ي changes to the consonant ـي (y) before the past tense suffixes are added.

For example, مِشِي (transliteration: miʃii; meaning: to walk / leave).

Personal Pronoun	مِشِي *miʃii* **to walk / leave**
هُوَّ huwwa he	مِشِي miʃii
هِيَّ heyya she	مِشْيِت miʃyit
هُمَّ humma they (d./p.)	مِشْيُوا miʃyu
إِنْتَ ?enta you (m. s.)	مِشِيت miʃiit

إِنْتِي	مِشِيتِي
?enti	miʃiiti
you (f. s.)	
إِنْتُو	مِشِيتُوا
?entu	miʃiitu
you (d./p.)	
أَنَا	مِشِيت
?ana	miʃiit
I	
إِحْنَا	مِشِينَا
?eħna	miʃiina
we	

Hollow Verbs (Verbs with Long Middle Vowels)

For a hollow verb (الفِعـل الأجـوف) with ١ *(?alif)* as the second letter, keep the ١ for third-person pronouns.

With first- and second-person pronouns, change the ١ to a short vowel according to these rules:

- If the middle root letter of the verb in the unmarked present (third-person masculine singular) is و (long 'uu'), then in the past tense delete the ١ (second letter) and put a *ḍamma* (short 'u') on the first letter.
  For example, كـان, يـكون (transliteration: *kaan, yikuun*; meaning: to be).
- If the middle root letter of the verb in the unmarked present is ي (long 'ii'), then in the past tense delete the ١ (second letter) and put a *kasra* (short 'i') on the first letter.
  For example, سـاب, يـسـيب (transliteration: *saab, yisiib*; meaning: to leave / quit).

Personal Pronoun	كـان *kaan* to be	سـاب *saab* to leave behind / quit
هُوَّ huwwa he	كـان kaan	سـاب saab
هِيَّ heyya she	كـانِت kaanit	سـابِت saabit
هُمَّ humma they (d./p.)	كـانُوا kaanu	سـابُوا saabu
إِنْتَ ʔenta you (m. s.)	كُنْت kunt	سِبْت sibt
إِنْتِي ʔenti you (f. s.)	كُنْتِي kunti	سِبْتِي sibti
إِنْتُو ʔentu you (d./p.)	كُنْتُوا kuntu	سِبْتُوا sibtu
أنا ʔana I	كُنْت kunt	سِبْت sibt
إِحْنـا ʔeḥna we	كُنَّـا kunna	سِبْنـا sibna

Exception: The Verb جَه (gah)

Although جَه (transliteration: gah; meaning: to come) is made up of
two consonants, its conjugation in the affirmative form differs from
similar verbs in the same group, such as كَل (transliteration: kal;
meaning: to eat).

As shown in the following table, to conjugate جَه drop the final ـه
(h) and add the sound 'ee' (as the 'ai' in the English word 'straight')
before adding the past tense suffixes with the first- and second-
person pronouns; for the pronoun هِيّ (heyya), drop the final ـه (h)
before adding the past tense suffix; and for the pronoun هُمّ (humma),
switch the final ـه (h) to a م (m).

Personal Pronoun	جَه gah to come
هُوَّ huwwa he	جَه gah
هِيّ heyya she	جَت gat
هُمّ humma they (d./p.)	جُم gum
إنْتَ ʔenta you (m. s.)	جِيت geet
إنْتِي ʔenti you (f. s.)	جِيتِي geeti

إِنْتُو ʔentu you (d./p.)	جِيتُوا geetu
أَنا ʔana I	جِيت geet
إِحْنا ʔeħna we	جِينا geena

Exercise 1
Choose the correct form of the verb for each sentence.

Example:

إِنْتِي ـــــــــ هِدِيَّة إِمْبارِح.
(جِبْت – جِبْتِي – جابِت)

١- إِحْنا ـــــــــ الْفيِلْم فِي السِّينِما.
(شُفْنا – شُفْتُوا – شافِت)

٢- إِنْتُو ـــــــــ الْفاكْهَة إِمْبارِح.
(اِشْتَرُوا – اِشْتَرِيتُوا – اِشْتَرِينا)

٣- لَيْلَى ـــــــــ بَدْرِي.
(صِحِيتِي – صِحْيِت – صِحِيت)

٤- أَصْحابِي ـــــــــ مُدِير الْجامْعَة.
(قابِلْنا – قابِلْتُوا – قابْلُوا)

٥- أَنا ـــــــــ مَعانِي الْمُفْرَدات الْجِّدِيدَة.
(اِتْعَلَّم – اِتْعَلِّمِت – اِتْعَلَّمْت)

٦- يُوسِف _____ فِي الْمَطْعَم الْجَّدِيد.
(اِتْغَدَّى – اِتْغَدَّت – اِتْغَدِّيت)

٧- إِنْتِي _____ شَرْم الشِّيخ.
(سافَرْت – سافِرْت – سافِرْتِي)

٨- أَنـا _____ فُلُوس مِن أُخْتِي.
(اِسْتَلَفْت – اِسْتَلَفِت – اِسْتَلَف)

٩- إِنْتُو _____ سَمَك.
(اِتْعَشَّى – اِتْعَشِّيتُوا – اِتْعَشُّوا)

١٠- إِنْتَ _____ عَلَى شَقَّة جِدِيدَة.
(اِتْفَرَّجْت – اِتْفَرَّجْتِي – اِتْفَرَّج)

Exercise 2
Complete each sentence by conjugating the verb provided.

Example:

أَنـا (راح) شُغْلِي بِالْبـاص. أَنـا رُحْت شُغْلِي بِالْبـاص.

١- إِحْنـا _____ الشُّغْل فِي الشَّرْكَة. (ساب)

٢- هِيَّ _____ الجَّامْعَة إِمْبـارِح. (جَه)

٣- إِنْتِي _____ مَع صـاحْبِتِك فِي التَّلِيفُون. (اِتْكَلِّم)

٤- أَنـا _____ تـاكْسِي لِلجَّامْعَة. (رِكِب)

٥- هُمَّ _____ مَع الْمُدِير الجَّدِيد. (فِطِر)

٦- إِنْتَ _____ الْقَطْر. (لِحِق)

٧- بـابـاه _____ إِسْكِنْدِرِيَّة مِن أُسْبُوع. (سـافِر)

٨- لَيْلَى وسَلْوَى _____ حَفْلِةْ عِيد مِيلاد صَاحْبِتْهُم. (راح)

٩- إنْتُو _____ عِنْوان الشّرْكَة. (عِرِف)

١٠- أنَا _____ مَعَاد الدُّكْتُور. (نِسِي)

Exercise 3

Tell your classmates what you did in each of the following places, using as many past tense verbs as you can.

١- الْبَنْك
٢- الجَّامْعَة
٣- السِّينِما
٤- الْمُسْتَشْفَى
٥- السُّوبَر مارْكِت

Exercise 4

Talk about your first experience in each of the following situations.

1. Driving a car.
2. Learning a foreign language.
3. Traveling outside your country.
4. Attending a job interview.
5. Renting an apartment.
6. Celebrating a birthday, festival, holiday, or other special occasion.

Lesson 15: Negation of Past Tense Verbs

Verbs of Two, Three, or More Consonants with *Fatha*

As shown in the following table, the prefix مَ *(ma)* and the suffix ش *(ʃ)* are used to negate:

- Verbs consisting of two consonants where the first consonant has a *fatha* (short 'a')—for example, كَل (transliteration: *kal*; meaning: to eat).
- Verbs of three consonants with a *fatha* on the first and second consonants—for example, خَرَج (transliteration: *xarag*; meaning: to go out / leave).
- Verbs of more than three consonants with a *fatha* on the first or middle consonants—for example, خَلَص (transliteration: *xallaṣ*; meaning: to finish).

Note that since three consonants in a row are not acceptable in Arabic, a *kasra* (short 'i') should be inserted before the suffix ش *(ʃ)* when needed, as with the pronouns أنا *(ʔana)* and إنْتَ *(ʔenta)*.

Personal Pronoun	كَل *kal* Negative Form	خَرَج *xarag* Negative Form	خَلَص *xallaṣ* Negative Form
هُوَّ huwwa He	مكَلْش makalʃ	مخَرَجْش maxaragʃ	مخَلَصْش maxallaṣʃ
هِيَّ heyya She	مكَلِتْش makalitʃ	مخَرَجِتْش maxaragitʃ	مخَلَصِتْش maxallaṣitʃ
هُمَّ humma they (d./p.)	مكَلُوش makaluuʃ	مخَرَجُوش maxaraguuʃ	مخَلَصُوش maxallaṣuuʃ
إنْتَ ʔenta you (m. s.)	مكَلْتِش makaltiʃ	مخَرَجْتِش maxaragtiʃ	مخَلَصْتِش maxallaṣtiʃ

إِنْتِي ʔenti you (f. s.)	مـكَـلْتِـيش makaltiiʃ	مـخَـرَجْتِـيش maxaragtiiʃ	مـخَـلَّـصْـتِـيش maxallaṣtiiʃ
إِنْتُو ʔentu you (d./p.)	مـكَـلْتُـوش makaltuuʃ	مـخَـرَجْـتُـوش maxaragtuuʃ	مـخَـلَّـصْـتُـوش maxallaṣtuuʃ
أَنـا ʔana I	مـكَـلْـتِـش makaltiʃ	مـخَـرَجْـتِـش maxaragtiʃ	مـخَـلَّـصْـتِـش maxallaṣtiʃ
إِحْنـا ʔeḥna we	مـكَـلْنـاش makalnaaʃ	مـخَـرَجْنـاش maxaragnaaʃ	مـخَـلَّـصْنـاش maxallaṣnaaʃ

Verbs Starting with ﺍ *(ʔalif)*

To negate verbs starting with ﺍ *(ʔalif)*, the ﺍ should be dropped before adding the prefix مَ *(ma)* and the suffix ش *(ʃ)*.

For example اِتْكَـلَّـم (transliteration: *itkallim*; meaning: to speak / talk), as shown in the following table.

Personal Pronoun	اِتْكَـلَّـم *itkallim* **Negative Form**
هُـوَّ huwwa he	مـتْـكَـلِّـمْـش matkallimʃ
هِـيَّ heyya she	مـتْـكَـلِّـمِـتْـش matkallimitʃ

هُمَّ humma they (d./p.)	مـتْـكَـلْـمُـوش matkallimuuʃ
إنْـتَ ʔenta you (m. s.)	مـتْـكَـلْـمْـتِـش matkallimtiʃ
إنْـتِـي ʔenti you (f. s.)	مـتْـكَـلْـمْـتِـيش matkallimtiiʃ
إنْـتُـو ʔentu you (d./p.)	مـتْـكَـلْـمْـتُـوش matkallimtuuʃ
أنـا ʔana I	مـتْـكَـلْـمْـتِـش matkallimtiʃ
إحْـنـا ʔeħna we	مـتْـكَـلْـمْـنـاش matkallimnaaʃ

Verbs Conjugated like شِـرِب (ʃirib)

As shown in the following table, when negating verbs conjugated like شِـرِب (transliteration: ʃirib; meaning: to drink), add the prefix مَ (ma) and the suffix ش (ʃ). For all pronouns except هِـيَّ (heyya) and هُـمَّ (humma), then drop the kasra (short 'i') below the first consonant.

Personal Pronoun	شِرِب *ʃirib* Negative Form
هُوَّ huwwa he	مـشْـرِبْـش maʃribʃ
هِـيَّ heyya she	مـشِـرْبِـتْـش maʃirbitʃ
هُـمَّ humma they (d./p.)	مـشِـرْبُـوش maʃirbuuʃ
إِنْـتَ ʔenta you (m. s.)	مـشْـرِبْـتِـش maʃribtiʃ
إِنْـتِـي ʔenti you (f. s.)	مـشْـرِبْـتِـيش maʃribtiiʃ
إِنْـتُـو ʔentu you (d./p.)	مـشْـرِبْـتُـوش maʃribtuuʃ
أنـا ʔana I	مـشْـرِبْـتِـش maʃribtiʃ
إِحْـنـا ʔeħna we	مـشِـرْبْـنـاش maʃribnaaʃ

Verbs of Two Consonants with a Second Consonant Doubled

As shown in the following table, for verbs with a *fadda* (doubling) on the second consonant, add the prefix مَ *(ma)* and the suffix ش *(ʃ)*. For all pronouns except هِيَّ *(heyya)* and هُمَّ *(humma)*, then drop the 'ee' sound (like the 'ai' in 'straight') that is added in the affirmative conjugation.

For example, بَصّ (transliteration: *baṣṣ*; meaning: to look)

Personal Pronoun	بَصّ *baṣṣ* Negative Form
هُوَّ huwwa he	مـَبَصّـِش mabaṣṣiʃ
هِيَّ heyya she	مـَبَصّـِتْش mabaṣṣitʃ
هُمَّ humma they (d./p.)	مـَبَصّـُوش mabaṣṣuuʃ
إِنْتَ ʔenta you (m. s.)	مـَبَصّـِتْش mabaṣṣitʃ
إِنْتِي ʔenti you (f. s.)	مـَبَصّـِتِيش mabaṣṣitiiʃ
إِنْتُو ʔentu you (d./p.)	مـَبَصّـُتُوش mabaṣṣituuʃ

أنا ʔana I	مبَصِّتْش mabaṣṣitʃ
إحْنا ʔeħna we	مبَصِّناش mabaṣṣinaaʃ

Verbs Ending with ى (ʔalif maksuura)

As shown in the following table, for verbs ending with ى (ʔalif maksuura, 'broken a') add the prefix مَ (ma) and the suffix ش (ʃ). For all pronouns except هِيَّ (heyya) and هُمَّ (humma), then drop the 'ee' sound (like the 'ai' in 'straight') that is added in the affirmative conjugation.

For example, اسْتَنَّى (transliteration: istanna; meaning: to wait (for).

Personal Pronoun	اسْتَنَّى istanna Negative Form
هُوَّ huwwa he	مسْتَنَّاش mastannaaʃ
هِيَّ heyya she	مسْتَنِّتْش mastannitʃ
هُمَّ humma they (d./p.)	مسْتَنُّوش mastannuuʃ

إِنْتَ	مَسْتَنِّتْش
?enta	mastannit∫
you (m. s.)	
إِنْتِي	مَسْتَنِّتِيش
?enti	mastannitii∫
you (f. s.)	
إِنْتُو	مَسْتَنِّتُوش
?entu	mastannituu∫
you (d./p.)	
أَنَا	مَسْتَنِّتْش
?ana	mastannit∫
I	
إِحْنَا	مَسْتَنِّنَاش
?eħna	mastanninaa∫
we	

Verbs Ending with ي (ya?)

As shown in the following table, for verbs ending with ي (ya?, long 'ii'), put a *sukuun* (zero vowel) on the first consonant and shorten the ي, with all pronouns except هِيَّ (heyya) and هُمَّ (humma), then add the prefix مَ (ma) and the suffix ش (∫).

For example, مِشِي (transliteration: *mi∫ii*; meaning: to leave, walk),

Personal Pronoun	مِشِي *mi∫ii* Negative Form
هُوَّ	مَمْشِيش
huwwa	mam∫ii∫
he	

هِـيَّ heyya she	مـمِـشْـيِـتْـش mamiʃyitʃ
هُـمَّ humma they (d./p.)	مـمِـشْـيُـوش mamiʃyuuʃ
إِنْـتَ ʔenta you (m. s.)	مـمْـشِـتْـش mamʃitʃ
إِنْـتِـي ʔenti you (f. s.)	مـمْـشِـتِـيش mamʃitiiʃ
إِنْـتُـو ʔentu you (d./p.)	مـمْـشِـتُـوش mamʃituuʃ
أنـا ʔana I	مـمْـشِـتْـش mamʃitʃ
إحْـنـا ʔeħna we	مـمْـشِـنـاش mamʃinaaʃ

Hollow Verbs (with Long Middle Vowels)

As shown in the following table, a hollow verb (الـفـعـل الأجـوف) with a long middle ا (ʔalif) is negated by adding the prefix مَ (ma) and the suffix ش (ʃ) to the affirmative form.

For example, كان (transliteration: *kaan*; meaning: to be)

Personal Pronoun	كان *kaan*	
	Affirmative Form	Negative Form
هُوَّ huwwa he	كان kaan	مَكَنْش makanʃ
هِيَّ heyya she	كانِت kaanit	مَكَنِتْش makanitʃ
هُمَّ humma they (d./p.)	كانُوا kaanu	مَكَنُوش makanuuʃ
إِنْتَ ʔenta you (m. s.)	كُنْت kunt	مَكُنْتِش makuntiʃ
إِنْتِي ʔenti you (f. s.)	كُنْتِي kunti	مَكُنْتِيش makuntiiʃ
إِنْتُو ʔentu you (d./p.)	كُنْتُوا kuntu	مَكُنْتُوش makuntuuʃ
أَنـا ʔana I	كُنْت kunt	مَكُنْتِش makuntiʃ
إِحْنـا ʔeħna we	كُنّـا kunna	مَكُنّـاش makunnaaʃ

Exception: The Verb جَه *(gah)*

Unlike other verbs of two consonants, the verb جَه (transliteration: *gah*; meaning: to come) has a different conjugation in both its affirmative and negative forms. To negate this verb, drop the 'ee' sound (like the 'ai' in 'straight') that is added in the affirmative conjugation with first- and second-person pronouns, then add the prefix مَ *(ma)* and the suffix ش *(ʃ)*. For the pronoun هِيَّ *(heyya)*, add the prefix مَ *(ma)* and the suffix ش *(ʃ)* to the affirmative form without any other changes.

The pronouns هُوَّ *(huwwa)* and هُمَّ *(humma)* are different and are are shown in the following table.

Personal Pronoun	جَه *gah*	
	Affirmative Form	**Negative Form**
هُوَّ huwwa he	جَه gah	مَجَاش magaaʃ
هِيَّ heyya she	جَت gat	مَجَتْش magatʃ
هُمَّ humma they (d./p.)	جُم gum	مَجُوش maguuʃ
إِنْتَ ʔenta you (m. s.)	جِيت geet	مَجِتْش magitʃ
إِنْتِي ʔenti you (f. s.)	جِيتِي geeti	مَجِتِيش magitiiʃ

إنْتُو ʔentu you (d./p.)	جِيتُوا geetu	مَجِتُوش magituuʃ
أنَا ʔana I	جِيت geet	مَجِتْش magitʃ
إحْنـا ʔeħna we	جِينـا geena	مَجِنـاش maginaaʃ

Exercise 1
Choose the correct conjugation for each sentence.

Example:

إحْنـا (مرُحْتُوش – مِرُحْنـاش – مرِحُوش) الجَامْعَة إمْبارِح.

١- هِيَّ (موَطِّتْش – موَطَّتِيش – موَطَّاش) صُـوت الرادْيُـو.

٢- إنْتِي (محَسِّتْش – محَسّش – محَسِّتِيش) بصُداع.

٣- إنْتُو (مدَفَعْتُوش – مدفَعُوش – مدفَعْنـاش) إيجار الشَّقَّة.

٤- هُوَّ (معَلِّتْش – معَلَّاش – معَلِّتِيش) صُوتُه قُدّام مُدِيرُه.

٥- إحْنـا (مقَبَضْتُوش – مقَبَضُوش – مقَبَضْنـاش) مُرتَّب الشَّهْر دا.

٦- هُمَّ (ملَقُوش – ملَقِتُوش – ملَقِنـاش) الفُلُوس اللّي ضـاعِت.

٧- أنـا (مدِّتِيش – مدّتْش – مدّاش) المقـالة للأستـاذ.

٨- سَلْوَى (مكِسْبِتْش – مكِسْبِتِيش – مكِسْبِتْش) في مبـاراةُ التِّنِس.

٩ـ هُوَّ لِسَّه (مِنَضَّفْتِيش – مِنَضَّفْش – مِنَضَّفِتْش) العربِيَّة.

١٠ـ إنْتَ (مْلِعِبْش – مْلِعِبْتِيش – مْلِعِبْتِش) مِعاهُم كُورَة لِيه؟

Exercise 2

Negate each of the following sentences.

Example:

إحْنا **خَدْنا** أجازَة.
إحْنا **مَخَدْناش** أجازَة.

١ـ أنا قَرِيت كِتابِين.

_____

٢ـ لَيْلَى كَتَبِت مَقالة.

_____

٣ـ إحْنا لِعِبْنا تِنِس.

_____

٤ـ إنْتَ ذاكِرْت كِتِير إمْبارِح.

_____

٥ـ إنْتِي جِرِيتِي فِي النَّادِي.

_____

٦ـ أصْحابِي سِكْنُوا فِي نَفْس الشَّارِع.

_____

٧ـ إنْتُو دَرَسْتُوا لُغات مُخْتَلِفَة.

_____

٨ـ أنا فِهِمْت الْمَوْضُوع.

_____

٩- إنْتِي صَرَفْتِي فُلُوس كتِير فِي السُّوبَر مارْكِت.

_____

١٠- مامِتْها جابِت لَها هِدِيّةُ عِيد مِيلادْها.

_____

> **Exercise 3**
> Extract all the past tense verbs from the following passage
> and then negate them.

حَلّ	مُشكِلةٌ	عَدِّيت عَلى
solving	problem	passed by
زِيارْتِي	وَرْد	القَرْض
my visit	flowers	Loan

يُوم الثَّلات صِحِيت السَّاعَة سِتَّة الصُّبْح. خَدتّ دُشّ وفِطِرْت وشِرِبْت قَهْوِتِي وقَرِيت الجُرْنال ولِبِست هُدُومِي. نِزِلْت مِن البِيت وسُقْت عَرِبِيّتِي وعَدِّيت عَلى صاحْبِي يُوسِف. رُحْنـا البِنْك واتكلمنا مع المدير ووعدنا يساعد في حلّ مشكلة القرض. بعد كده رحنا زرنا والد يوسف في المستشفى وخدت له ورد. والْدُه اتْبَسَط قَوِي مِن زِيارْتِي.

اتْغَدِّيت مَع يُوسِف فِي مطْعَم قُرَيِّب مِن الْمُسْتَشْفـى وبَعْدِين هُوَّ رِجِـع المُسْتَشْفَـى لِوالْدُه وأنـا عَدِّيت عَلى السُّوبَر مارْكِت واشْتَرِيت حـاجـات كِتِير لِلْبِيت. بَعْد الضُّهْـر رُحْت السِّينمـا مَع أوْلادِي ورِجِعْنـا اتْعَشِّينـا وقريت في كتاب شُوَيّة وبَعْدِين نِمْت.

Lesson 16: The Relative Pronoun

Form of the Relative Pronoun

Egyptian Colloquial Arabic has only one relative pronoun (الاسم الـمـوصـول): اللّـي *(illi)*. It is translated as 'who,' 'whom,' 'which,' 'that,' or 'whose,' depending on the context.

What Precedes the Relative Pronoun

The noun before the relative pronoun must be definite.

الـبِنْت الـلّـي فِـي الـفَـصْـل مَـصْـرِيَّـة.	ilbint-illi fi-ilfaşl maşriyya
The girl who is in the class is Egyptian.	

The relative pronoun can also be preceded by an interrogative.

مِـين الـلّـي فِـي الـبِـيت دِلْـوَقتِـي؟	miin-illi fi-ilbeet dilwaʔti
Who is in the house now?	

What Follows the Relative Pronoun

The relative pronoun can be followed by any of these:
- **A verbal sentence**

الـسِّـتّ الـلّـي جَـت الـحـفـلـة جمـيـلـة.	issitt-illi gat-il ħafla gamiila
The woman who came to the party is beautiful.	

- **A prepositional phrase**

الـمـطـعـم الـلّـي قـدَّام بـيـتـي كبـيـر.
ilmaʈʒam-illi ʔuddaam beeti kibiir
The restaurant which is in front of my house is big.
الـشـقـة الـلّـي فـي الـدور الـتـانـي غـالـيـة.
iʃʃaʔʔa-lli fi-ddoor-ittaani ɣalya
The apartment that is on the second floor is expensive.

Pronominal suffixes

When using the relative pronoun, a pronominal suffix is often attached to a preposition or verb so as to refer to the main subject of the sentence. This is done if there is more than one subject in the sentence.

الشَّقَّة اللّي عِشْت فيها كانت كِبِيرَة.
iʃʃaʔʔa-lli ʒiʃt fiiha kaanit kibiira
The apartment in which I lived was big.
الْمُدَرِّس اللّي كَلِّمْناه إمْبارِح سافِر النَّهارْده الصُّبْح.
ilmudarris-illi kallimnaah-imbaariħ saafir-innahaarda-ṣṣubħ
The teacher to whom we spoke yesterday traveled this morning.

Exercise 1
Mark each sentence as correct or incorrect, and rewrite those that are incorrect.

Example:

(√) الشَّنطة اللّي مع مها جديدة.
(X) السَّاعَة اللّي اِشْتَريت كانِت غالْيَة قَوي.
السّاعة اللّي اشتريتها كانت غالية قوي.

_____

١ـ أصْحابِي اللّي معايا في الجَّامْعَة لِبْنانِيِّين.

_____

٢ـ البِنْت اللّي قابِلْنا في الحفْلَة ساكْنَة في الشَّارِع دا.

_____

٣ـ المَطعَم اللّي كلِتُوا فِي مِش غالِي.

_____

٤ـ العربِيَّة اللّي اِشْتراها عَمّي لُونْها أحْمَر.

_____

٥- الْبَنَات اللِّي كَانُوا قُدَّام النَّادِي مِشْيُوا من شُوَيَّة.

_____

٦- إِنْتِي كَتَبْتِي الْمَقَالَة اللِّي طَوِيلَة.

_____

٧- الرَّحْلَة اللِّي رُحْتَّها كَانِت جَمِيلَة.

_____

٨- الْقَمِيص اللِّي يُوسِف لِبِس في الْحَفْلَة شِيك خَالِص.

_____

٩- شُفْتُوا فِي النَّادِي الْفَرِيق اللِّي أَسْبَانِي؟

_____

١٠- الكُّمْبِيُوتَر اللِّي بِتَاعُها سِعْرُه حِلْو.

_____

Exercise 2
Connect each pair of sentences using اللِّي.

Example:

هُوَّ كَتَب جَواب. الْجَواب كان طَوِيل.
الْجَواب اللِّي كَتَبُه كان طَوِيل.

١- أنَا اِشْتَرِيت قامُوس. الْقامُوس غالِي.

_____

٢- هِيّ عَنْدَها فُلُوس. الْفُلُوس فِي البَنْك.

_____

٣- إحْنا قَعَدْنا فِي أوتِيل. الأوتِيل مِش ٥ نُجُوم.

_____

٤- الْمُدِير عَمَل حَفْلَة. أنا رُحْت الْحَفْلَة.

_____

٥ـ هُمَّ بـاعُوا الشَّقَّة. الشَّقَّة فيها حَمَّامِين.

_____

٦ـ لَيْلَى لِبْست بِلُوزَة. البِلُوزَة لُونْها أَخْضَر.

_____

٧ـ إنْتُو خَلَّصْتُوا الدُّرُوس. الدُّرُوس مكنِتْش صَعْبَة.

_____

٨ـ يُوسِف دَخَل الجَّامْعَة. الجَّامْعَة بِعِيدَة عَن بِيتُه.

_____

٩ـ نِسِيت المَعـاد. المَعـاد كـان مُهِمّ قَوِي.

_____

١٠ـ زُرْنـا بِلاد كِتِيرَة. البِلاد كـانِت فِي أُورُوبَّا.

_____

Exercise 3
Write a sentence that uses اللِّي and starts with the word provided.

Example:

الطَّالِبَة
الطَّالِبَة اللَّي قابِلْناها فِي الجَّامْعَة إمبارح كِويتِيّة.

_____

١ـ الجَّامْعَة

_____

٢ـ خـالِي

_____

٣ـ النَّضَّارَة

_____

٤ـ الدُّكْتُورَة

_____

٥ـ العَرَبِيَّة

_____

٦ـ القَمِيص

٧- الـبِـنْـتِـين _____

٨- الأسـاتِـذَة _____

٩- الـكُـتُـب _____

١٠- أصْـحـابُـه _____

Lesson 17: The Unmarked Present

How to Form the Unmarked Present (الـفـعل الـمـضـارع)

This tense is formed by adding certain prefixes and suffixes to the past tense form for the pronoun هُوَّ *(huwwa)*, as explained below.

⤷ **Sound verbs without long vowels in their present tense forms**
For example, يِشْرَب (transliteration: *yiʃrab*; meaning: to drink)

Personal Pronoun	يِشْرَب *yiʃrab*
هُوَّ huwwa he	يِشْرَب yiʃrab
هِـيَّ heyya she	تِشْرَب tiʃrab
هُمَّ humma they (d./p.)	يِشْرَبُوا yiʃrabu
إِنْتَ ʔenta you (m. s.)	تِشْرَب tiʃrab
إِنْتِـي ʔenti you (f. s.)	تِشْرَبِي tiʃrabi
إِنْتُـو ʔentu you (d./p.)	تِشْرَبُوا tiʃrabu
أنـا ʔana I	أشْرَب ʔaʃrab

إِحْنـا ʔeħna we	نِـشْـرَب niʃrab

◟ Sound verbs with different voweling

If the prefix ـِ *(y)* for present tense form of the pronoun هُوَّ *(huwwa)* has a *ḍamma* (short 'u'), then the prefixes for all other pronouns also have a *ḍamma*, except for the pronoun أنـا *(ʔana)*.

For example, يُخْرُج (transliteration: *yuxrug*; meaning to leave / go out).

Personal Pronoun	يُخْرُج *yuxrug*
هُوَّ huwwa he	يُخْرُج yuxrug
هِيَّ heyya she	تُخْرُج tuxrug
هُمَّ humma they (d./p.)	يُخْرُجُوا yuxrugu
إِنْتَ ʔenta you (m. s.)	تُخْرُج tuxrug
إِنْتِي ʔenti you (f. s.)	تُخْرُجِي tuxrugi
إِنْتُو ʔentu you (d./p.)	تُخْرُجُوا tuxrugu

أَنَا	أَخْرُج
?ana	?axrug
I	

إِحْنَا	نُخْرُج
?ehna	nuxrug
we	

◟ Weak verbs
▦ Verbs ending with long vowels in the present tense
In verbs ending with ى (?alif maksuura, 'broken a'), drop the ى
when conjugating the present tense for the pronouns هُمَّ (humma),
إِنْتِي (?enti), and إِنْتُو (?entu). For example, يِسْتَنَّى (transliteration:
yistanna; meaning: he waits (for)).

In verbs ending with ي (ya?), drop the ي when conjugating the
present tense for the pronouns هُمَّ (humma), إِنْتِي (?enti), and إِنْتُو
(?entu). For example, يِمْشِي (transliteration: yimʃii; meaning: he
walks / leaves).

Personal Pronoun	يِسْتَنَّى yistanna	يِمْشِي yimʃii
هُوَّ huwwa he	يِسْتَنَّى yistanna	يِمْشِي yimʃii
هِيَّ heyya she	تِسْتَنَّى tistanna	تِمْشِي timʃii
هُمَّ humma they (d./p.)	يِسْتَنُّوا yistannu	يِمْشُوا yimʃu
إِنْتَ ?enta you (m. s.)	تِسْتَنَّى tistanna	تِمْشِي timʃii

إِنْتِي ʔenti you (f. s.)	تِسْتَنِّي tistanni	تِمْشِي timʃii
إِنْتُو ʔentu you (d./p.)	تِسْتَنُّوا tistannu	تِمْشُوا timʃu
أَنَا ʔana I	أَسْتَنَّى ʔastanna	أَمْشِي ʔamʃii
إِحْنَا ʔeħna we	نِسْتَنَّى nistanna	نِمْشِي nimʃii

▨ Verbs where ا (ʔalif) follows the ـ (ya) prefix

In verbs where ا (ʔalif) follows the ـ (ya) prefix that is added to the present tense form for هُوَّ (huwwa), the consonant after the ا has a *sukuun* (zero vowel) when conjugating for the pronouns هُمَّ (humma), إِنْتِي (ʔenti), and إِنْتُو (ʔentu) and the ا itself is deleted.

For example, يـاكُل (transliteration: *yaakul*; meaning: he eats).

Personal Pronoun	يـاكُل *yaakul*
هُوَّ huwwa he	يـاكُل yaakul
هِيَّ heyya she	تـاكُل taakul
هُمَّ humma they (d./p.)	يِكْلُوا yaklu

إِنْتَ ʔenta you (m. s.)	تَاكُل taakul
إِنْتِي ʔenti you (f. s.)	تَكْلِي takli
إِنْتُو ʔentu you (d./p.)	تَكْلُوا taklu
أَنَا ʔana I	آكُل ʔaakul
إِحْنَا ʔeħna we	نَاكُل naakul

Uses of the Unmarked Present
ꙭ To offer or suggest something or to give advice

تِشْرَب شَاي؟	tiʃrab ʃaay
Would you like to drink tea?	
أَيْوَه أَشْرَب.	ʔaywa-ʃrab
Yes, I would.	

Sometimes, two consecutive unmarked present tense verbs can be used together.

تِيجِي نْرُوح السِّينِمَا؟	tiigi-nruuħ-issinima
How about going to the cinema?	

After habitual verbs expressing ability or wishes

Unmarked present tense verbs can be used after habitual verbs that express ability or wishes. Habitual verbs are explained in lesson 19. In the following examples, the habitual verbs are underlined and the unmarked present tense verbs follow them.

بِيِقْدَر يِتْكَلَّم عَرَبِي بِسُرْعَة.	biyi?dar yitkallim ʒarabi-b-surʒa
He <u>can</u> speak Arabic fast.	
بـاعْرَف أَعُوم كُوَيِّس.	baʒraf-aʒuum kuwayyis
I <u>can</u> swim well.	
بِنْحِبّ نِسْمَع مُوسِيقَى.	binħibb-i-nismaʒ musiiqa
We <u>like</u> to listen to music.	
بـاتْمَنَّى أَكُون فنّـان مَشْـهُور.	batmanna ?akuun fannaan maʃhuur
I <u>hope</u> to become a famous artist.	

After future tense verbs

The unmarked present can be used after future tense verbs. Future tense verbs are explained in lesson 21 and are underlined in the following example.

حـاطْلَع أَتْكَلَّم مَعَ الْمُدِير.	ħatʃlaʒ ?atkallim maʒa-ilmudiir
I <u>will go</u> upstairs to talk to the manager.	

After past tense verbs

The unmarked present tense can be used after past tense verbs.

هُوَّ نِسِي يِعْمِل الـواجِـب.	huwwa nisi yiʒmil-ilwaagib
He <u>forgot</u> to do the homework.	

After the active participle

The unmarked present can be used after the active participle (الاسم الفاعل), which is explained in lesson 25 and which is underlined in the following examples.

هِيَّ عـايْزَة تِشْرَب شـاي.	heyya ʒayza tiʃrab ʃaay
She <u>wants</u> to drink tea.	
هُوَّ نـاوِي يِدْرِس عَرَبِي فِي الـخَـرِيف.	huwwa naawi yidris ʒarabi fi-ilxariif
He <u>intends</u> to learn Arabic in the fall.	
إحْنـا رايْحِين نِجِيب هِدِيَّة.	eḥna rayḥiin nigiib hediyya
We <u>are going</u> to get a gift.	

The active participle comes in three forms: the masculine, feminine, and dual / plural forms for both genders. For more detail, see the following table.

English Translation	Masculine Form	Feminine Form	Dual / Plural Form
Wanting	عـايِز ʒaayiz	عـايْزَة ʒayza	عـايْزِين ʒayziin
intending / planning (to)	نـاوِي naawi	نـاوْيَة nawya	نـاوْيِين nawyiin
going (to)	رايِح raayiḥ	رايْحَة rayḥa	رايْحِين rayḥiin

ꙫ After modals

Modals have fixed forms; they are never conjugated. The present tense following a modal is conjugated as usual. Modals are underlined in the following examples.

أنـا مُسْتَحِيل أسُوق الـعَرَبِيَّة بـالـلَيل.
ʔana mustaḥiil ʔasuuʔ-ilʒarabiyya billeel
It is <u>impossible</u> for me to drive the car at night.
هُمَّ مُمْكِن يِفْطَرُوا فِي مَطْعَم.
humma mumkin yifʈaru-f-maʈʒam

It is <u>possible</u> for them to have breakfast in a restaurant.
إحْنـا مُـهِـمّ نِقابِـل الْـمُـدِير.
eħna muhimm niʔaabil-ilmudiir
It is <u>important</u> that we meet the manager.
هُـوَّ مَفْـرُوض / ضَـرُورِي / لازِم يِشْـتِـري عَرَبِيَّـة.
huwwa mɑfruuḍ / ḍɑruuri / laazim yiʃtiri ӡɑrɑbiyya
It is <u>mandatory</u> / <u>essential</u> / <u>necessary</u> that he buys a car.
هِـيَّ يِـمْكِن / جايِـز / مُـحْـتَـمَل تِـرُوح الجَّـامْعَـة.
heyya yimkin / gaayiz / muħtamal tiruuħ-iggamӡa
It is <u>possible</u> / <u>likely</u> / <u>probably</u> that she goes to the university.

After connectors, nouns, particles, and phrases

عَشَـان (transliteration: *ӡaʃaan*; meaning: in order to / because)

راح السُّـوق عَشَـان يِشْـتِـري الـْخُـضـار.
rɑɑħ-issuuʔ ӡaʃaan yiʃtiri-ilxuḍɑɑr
He went to the market in order to buy vegetables.

يـارِيت (transliteration: *yareet*; meaning: hopefully)

أنـا يـارِيت أفْهَم الـدَّرْس.
ʔana yareet ʔafham-iddars
Hopefully, I will understand the lesson.

نِـفْس (*nifs*) + pronominal suffix (meaning: wish)

نِـفْسِي أسـافِر اليابـان.	nifsi ʔasaafir-ilyabaan
I wish to travel to Japan.	

حَقّ (ḥaʔʔ) + pronominal suffix (meaing: should / deserve)

حَقَّك تـاخُد أجـازَة عَشـان إنْتَ عَيَّان قَـوي.
ḥaʔʔak taaxud ʔagaaza ʒaʃaan-inta ʒayyaan ʔawi
You deserve to / It is your right to / You should (really) take a vacation because you are very sick.

يلَّا (transliteration: yalla; meaning: let's)

يلَّا نِقابِل الْمُدِير.	yalla-nʔaabil-ilmudiir
Let's meet the manager.	

مـا (transliteration: ma; meaning: why don't)

مـاتْرُوح لِلدُّكْتُور عشـان إنْتَ عيَّان قوي؟
matruuḥ lidduktoor ʒaʃaan-inta ʒayyaan ʔawi
Why don't you go to the doctor since you are very sick?

لمَّا (lamma) / وَقْت مـا (waʔt ma) (meaning: when)

لمَّا / وَقْت مـا تِروح الـجـامـعـة لازم تتكلَّم مـع الأستـاذ.
lamma / waʔt ma-truuḥ-iggamʒa laazim titkallim maʒa-ilʔustaaz
When you go to the university, you have to talk to the teacher.

قَبْل مـا (transliteration: ʔabli-ma; meaning: before)

قبـل مـا أسـافِر الْـيـابـان قَـريت عن الثَّـقـافَة الـيـابـانِـيَّـة.
ʔabli-masaafir-ilyabaan ʔareet ʒan-issaqaafa-ilyaabaaniyya
Before I traveled to Japan, I read about the Japanese culture.

بَعْد ما (transliteration: *baʒdi-ma*; meaning: after)

بـعد مـا نـخَلَّـص الـدَّرس يِمْكِن نِرُوح الْمَتْحَف.
baʒdi-manxallaṣṣ-iddars yimkin niruuḥ-ilmatḥaf
After we finish the lesson, we might go to the museum.

بَدَل ما (transliteration: *badal ma*; meaning: instead of)

بَدَل مـا تـروح الـسِّيـنِـمـا يـارِيت تِخـلَّـص واجِب الـعَرَبـِي الأوَّل.
badal matruuḥ-issinima yareet tixallaṣṣ wagib-ilʒarabi-il?awwal
Instead of going to the cinema, I hope you finish your Arabic homework first.

عَلَى قَدَ ما (transliteration: *ʒala ?addi-ma*; meaning: as much as)

عَلَى قَدَ مـا تِقْدَر مَفْروض تِسْأل عَلَى جِدَّك.
ʒala ?addi-mati?dar mafruuḍ tis?al ʒala giddak
You should ask about your grandfather as much as you can.

Exercise 1
Choose the correct conjugation for each sentence.

Example:

هِيَّ يِمْكِن (تِرُوحِي – تِرُوح – يِرُوح) مـعـانـا الـحَفْلَة.

١ـ أنـا يـارِيت (تِسـافِر – أسـافِر – تِسـافْرِي) لِبْـنـان فِي الأجـازَة.

٢ـ هُمْ عـايْزِين (يِشْتِـرُوا – نِشْتِـرِي – تِشْتِـروا) هُدُوم جِدِيدة.

٣ـ إحْـنـا لازِم (نِتْـغَدَّى – تِتْـغَدُّوا – يِتْـغَدَّى) مَع الـمُدِير بُكْرَة.

٤ـ إنْتِـي حَقَّك (يـاخُد – تـاخُد – تـاخْـدِي) الـفُلُوس مِنْـهُم.

٥- إِنْتُو يِمْكِن (يِشُوفُوا – تِشُوفُوا – نِشُوف) الفِيلْم فِي السِّينِمـا.

٦- هِيّ مِمْكِن (تِتْكَلِّم – أتْكَلِّم – تِتْكَلِّمِي) مع الأُسْتـاذ بعد الضُّهْر.

٧- إِنْتَ نِفْسَك (يِزُور – تِزُور – تِزُورِي) البَلَد دِي.

٨- أنا مِسْتَحِيل (نِبِيـع – تِبِيـع – أبِيـع) الشَّقَّة دِي.

٩- إحْنـا ضـرورِي (نذاكِر – تِذاكُرُوا – يِذاكُرُوا) كِتِير النَّهارْده.

١٠- هِي مُهِمّ (تِسْتَنِّي – تِسْتَنَّى – أَسْتَنَّى) ابْنهـا قُدَّام بـاب المَدْرَسَة.

Exercise 2
Complete each sentence by conjugating the two verbs provided.

Example:

أنـا (عِرِف + يِسُوق) عربيـة.
أنـا **عرفت أسوق** عربيـة.

١- إحْنـا (راح + يِشْتِرِي) كُتُب.

_____

٢- إنْتِي (قِدِر + يِتْعَلِّم) أَسْبانِي بِسُرْعَة.

_____

٣- هِيَّ (عِرِف + يِوْصَل) الجَّامْعَة.

_____

٤- إنْتُو (راح + يِتْكَلِّم) مَعَ المُدِير.

_____

٥- إنْتَ (قِدِر + يِصْحَى) بَدْرِي.

_____

٦- هُمَّ (عِرِف + يِسافِر) إسْكِنْدِرِيَّة.

_____

٧- أنا (راح + يِشُوف) الْفِيلْم فِي السِّينِما.

_____

٨- إنْتُو (قِدِر + يِتْغَدَّى) فِي الْمَطْعَم الْجِّدِيد.

_____

٩- إنْتِي (عِرِف + يُطْبُخ) أكْل مَصْرِي.

_____

١٠- إحْنا (قِدِر + يِخَلَّص) الشُّغْل كُلُّه.

_____

Exercise 3
Use modals and the unmarked present tense to give advice or to
comment on each of the following situations.

Example:

جار عايز يـأجَّر شقـة.
١- ضروري تسـأل عن سمسـار.
٢- لازم تتفرج على الشقـة كويس قبل مـا تأجِّرهـا.
٣- يمكن تحتاج تدفع فلوس مقدَّم.

_____

١- صديق عنده برد شديد من شهر ولسَّه مراحش للدكتـور.

٢- صديقة عندها مقابلـة لوظيفة جديدة لأول مرة في حيـاتهـا.

٣- صديق ساعدنا كتير والأسبوع دا حفلـة جوازه.

٤- صديق وصديقـة ليكو قرروا الطـلاق رغم إنـهم اتجوِّزوا بـعد
قصة حبّ طَويلـة.

٥- صديقة مهدَّدة بـالفصل من شغلها عشان أداءها مش كويس
وهِيّ محتاجَة جدًّا لشـغلهـا.

٦ـ صديق عنده صعوبة في فهم اللغة الإنجليزية وده ممكن يسبّب فشلُه في دراسته في الجامعة.

٧ـ عنده مؤتمر مهم جدًا في شرم الشيخ بس صعب يروح بسبب المطر وسوء حالة الجو.

٨ـ صديق أجنبي قرر يزور القاهرة لأول مرة بسّ مش عارف يروح فين.

٩ـ فيه صوت في شقة جيراننا مع إنهم مسافرين.

١٠ـ صديقة قالت إنها اتصلت بيك وماحدّش ردّ على التليفون مع إنك مخرجتش من البيت.

Lesson 18: Negation of the Unmarked Present

Sound Verbs

To negate a sound verb, add the prefix مَ *(ma)* and the suffix ش *(ʃ)* to the verb. For the pronoun أنـا *(ʔana)*, also drop the letter أ *(ʔa)*.

Personal Pronoun	Affirmative Form	Negative Form
هُوَّ huwwa he	يِشْرَب yiʃrab	مـيِشْرَبْش mayiʃrabʃ
هِيَّ heyya she	تِشْرَب tiʃrab	مَتِشْرَبْش matiʃrabʃ
هُمَّ humma they (d./p.)	يِشْرَبُوا yiʃrabu	مـيِشْرَبُوش mayiʃrabuuʃ
إنـت ʔenta you (m. s.)	تِشْرَب tiʃrab	مَتِشْرَبْش matiʃrabʃ
إنْتِـي ʔenti you (f. s.)	تِشْرَبِي tiʃrabi	مَتِشْرَبِيش matiʃrabiiʃ
إنْتُـو ʔentu you (d./p.)	تِشْرَبُوا tiʃrabu	مَتِشْرَبُوش matiʃrabuuʃ
أنـا ʔana I	أشْرَب ʔaʃrab	مَشْرَبْش maʃrabʃ
إحْنـا ʔeḥna we	نِشْرَب niʃrab	مَنِشْرَبْش maniʃrabʃ

Weak Verbs

For verbs ending with ى (*alif maksuura;* 'broken a'), replace the ى with an ا (long 'aa').

Personal Pronoun	Affirmative Form	Negative Form
هُوَّ huwwa he	يِسْتَنَّى yistanna	مِيسْتَنَّاش mayistannaaʃ
هِيَّ heyya she	تِسْتَنَّى tistanna	مَتِسْتَنَّاش matistannaaʃ
هُمَّ humma they (d./p.)	يِسْتَنُّوا yistannu	مِيسْتَنُّوش mayistannuuʃ
إنْت ʔenta you (m. s.)	تِسْتَنَّى tistanna	مَتِسْتَنَّاش matistannaaʃ
إنْتِي ʔenti you (f. s.)	تِسْتَنِّي tistanni	مَتِسْتَنِّيش matistanniiʃ
إنْتُو ʔentu you (d./p.)	تِسْتَنُّوا tistannu	مَتِسْتَنُّوش matistannuuʃ
أنا ʔana I	أسْتَنَّى ʔastanna	مسْتَنَّاش mastannaaʃ
إحْنا ʔeħna we	نِسْتَنَّى nistanna	مَنِسْتَنَّاش manistannaaʃ

Hollow Verbs with Long Middle Vowels and Verbs Ending in Double Consonants

Hollow verbs such as يِزُور (transliteration: *yizuur*; meaning: to visit) and verbs ending with double consonants such as يِحِبّ (transliteration: *yiħibb*; meaning: to like / love) are negated as explained below and shown in the following table.

For hollow verbs, shorten the long vowels, drop the *kasra* (short 'i') from the first consonant, and leave *sukuun* (zero vowel) on the prefix for all the pronouns except أنا *(ʔana)*. Then, add the prefix مَ *(ma)* and the suffix ش *(ʃ)*.

Personal Pronoun	Affirmative Form	Negative Form	Affirmative Form	Negative Form
هُوَّ huwwa he	يِزُور yizuur	مَيْزُرْش mayzurʃ	يِحِبّ yiħibb	مَيْحِبّش mayħibbiʃ
هِيَّ heyya she	تِزُور tizuur	مَتْزُرْش matzurʃ	تِحِبّ tiħibb	مَتْحِبّش matħibbiʃ
هُمَّ humma they (d./p.)	يِزُورُوا yizuuru	مَيْزُرُوش mayzuruuʃ	يِحِبُّوا yiħibbu	مَيْحِبُّوش mayħibbuuʃ
إِنْتَ ʔenta you (m. s.)	تِزُور tizuur	مَتْزُرْش matzurʃ	تِحِبّ tiħibb	مَتْحِبّش matħibbiʃ
إِنْتِي ʔenti you (f. s.)	تِزُورِي tizuuri	مَتْزُرِيش matzuriiʃ	تِحِبِّي tiħibbi	مَتْحِبِّيش matħibbiiʃ
إِنْتُو ʔentu you (d./p.)	تِزُورُوا tizuuru	مَتْزُرُوش matzuruuʃ	تِحِبُّوا tiħibbu	مَتْحِبُّوش matħibbuuʃ
أنا ʔana I	أزُور ʔazuur	مَزُرْش mazurʃ	أحِبّ ʔaħibb	مَحِبّش maħibbiʃ

إحْنا ʔeḥna we	نِزُور nizuur	مِنْزُرْش manzurʃ	نِحِبّ niḥibb	مِنْحِبِّش manḥibbiʃ

Exercise 1
Choose the correct conjugation for each sentence.

Example:

إنْتَ ضَرُوري (مِرُحْش – مِتْرُحْش – مِيْرُحْش) النَّادِي النَّهارْدَه.

١- إحْنا نِفْسِنا (مِنْبِعْش – مِبِعْش – مِيْبِعْش) بِيتْنا.

٢- إنْتِي ضروري (مِيجْرِيش – مِتِجْرِيش – مِجْرِيش) عشان إنْتِي تَعْبانَة.

٣- هِيَّ يمكن (مِتِرْجَعِيش – مِرْجَعْش – مِتِرْجَعْش) البيت بَدْري.

٤- إنْتُو جايِز (مِنْخَلَصْش – مِتْخَلَّصُوش – مِيْخَلَّصُوش) شُغْلُكُو دِلوقتِي.

٥- أنا ياريت (مِدْفَعْش – مِتِدْفَعْش – مِتِدفعِيش) الفاتُورة بكرة.

٦- إحْنا حقَّنا (مِتاخُدُوش – مِياخْدُوش – مِناخُدْش) أجازة دلوقتِي.

٧- إنْتَ يمكن (مِيتْغَدَّاش – مِتِتْغَدَّاش – مِتْغَدَّاش) مَعاهُم.

٨- أنا لازِم (مِيْسِبِش – مِتْسِبْش – مِسِبْش) الوظيفة دِي.

٩- هُمَ يمكن (مِيْقُلوش – مِتْقُلُوش – مِنْقُلْش) الحقيقة.

١٠- هِيَّ ياريت (مِقبِلْش – مِتْقَبِلْش – مِتْقبْلِيش) صاحب البيت هنا.

Exercise 2
State three things that you should not do in each of the following situations.

Example:

لَيْلَى عنْدَها امْتِحان مُهِمّ بُكْرَة.

١- لازِم مِتُخْرُجْش مِن البِيت.

٢- مفْرُوض مِتِتْفَرَّجْش عَلَى التِّلِيفِزْيُون.

٣- مُهِمّ مِتِتْكَلِّمْش فِي التِّلِيفُون.

١- بُكْرَة عنْدنا سَفَر طَوِيل.

٢- الأسْبُوع الـجَايّ عَنْدُهم ضُيُوف كِتِير.

٣- بعد بُكْرَة عَنْدكُو حفْلَة لمدير الشركة الجديد.

٤- عنْدُه مـعـاد مـع مدِير البنك عشـان عايز قـرْض.

٥- عَنْدِي افتتاح لمحَلِّي الجديد.

Lesson 19: Conjugation of Habitual Verbs

Habitual verbs (الفعل المضارع الذي يعبر عن عادة والفعل المضارع المستمر) are used to express what one does every day or what one is doing at the moment of speaking.

Sound Verbs

Sound verbs—those that do not have long vowels—are conjugated by adding a prefix ـِب *(bi)* to the unmarked present for all pronouns except أنا *(ʔana)*. With the pronoun أنا, change the prefix أ *(ʔa)* of the unmarked present to the prefix ـَب *(ba)*.

For example, بِيِشْرَب شاي (transliteration: *biyiʃrab ʃaay*; meaning: he drinks tea / he is drinking tea).

Personal Pronoun	Habitual Verb بِيِشْرَب
هُوَّ huwwa he	بِيِشْرَب biyiʃrab
هِيَّ heyya she	بِتِشْرَب bitiʃrab
هُمَّ humma they (d./p.)	بِيِشْرَبُوا biyiʃrabu
إِنْتَ ʔenta you (m. s.)	بِتِشْرَب bitiʃrab
إِنْتِي ʔenti you (f. s.)	بِتِشْرَبِي bitiʃrabi

إِنْتُو ʔentu you (d./p.)	بِتِشْرَبُوا bitiʃrabu
أَنَا ʔana I	بَشْرَب baʃrab
إِحْنَا ʔeħna we	بِنِشْرَب biniʃrab

Weak Verbs

In weak verbs- –hollow verbs or verbs ending with double consonants—the prefix of the unmarked present keeps the *sukuun* (zero vowel), for all pronouns except أَنَا *(ʔana)*. Add the prefix بَ *(ba)* to the pronoun أَنَا and the prefix بِ *(bi)* to all other pronouns.

For example, بِيْذاكِر (transliteration: *biyzaakir*; translation: he studies / he is studying); بِيْحُطّ (transliteration: *biyħuṭṭ*; meaning: he puts / he is putting).

Personal Pronoun	Habitual Verb بِيْذاكِر	Habitual Verb بِيْحُطّ
هُوَّ huwwa he	بِيْذاكِر biyzaakir	بِيْحُطّ biyħuṭṭ
هِيَّ heyya she	بِتْذاكِر bitzaakir	بِتْحُطّ bitħuṭṭ
هُمَّ humma they (d./p.)	بِيْذاكُرُوا biyzakru	بِيْحُطُّوا biyħuṭṭu

إِنْتَ ʔenta you (m. s.)	بِتْذاكِر bitzaakir	بِتْحُطّ bitḥuṭṭ
إِنْتِي ʔenti you (f. s.)	بِتْذاكْري bitzakri	بِتْحُطّي bitḥuṭṭi
إِنْتُو ʔentu you (d./p.)	بِتْذاكْرُوا bitzakru	بِتْحُطُّوا bitḥuṭṭu
أَنا ʔana I	بَذاكِر bazaakir	بَحُطّ baḥuṭṭ
إِحْنا ʔeḥna we	بِنْذاكِر binzaakir	بِنْحُطّ binḥuṭṭ

Exercise 1
Choose the correct conjugation for each sentence.

Example:

أنـا (بـفْطَر – بِيِفْطَر – بِتِفْطَر) فِي الشُّغْل كُلّ يُوم.

١- هُمَّ دايْمًا (بِيسْتعمِلوا – بتستعمِلُوا – بنستعمِل) الغسَّالة الكـهربـائيَّة.

٢- هِيَّ (بْتْفَرَّج – بِتِتْفرَّج – بتتفرَّجي) علـى التليفزيون كُلّ يُوم بـاللَّيـل.

٣- إنْتُو (بِتِسِتَنُّوا – بنـسـتَنَّـى – بِيسْتَنُّوا) الأُتوبِيس قُدام بـاب الـجـامـعـة.

٤- إِنْتِي (بخسَر – بتخسَر – بِتِخْسَري) فُلوس كتير في البـورصـة.

٥- أنـا (بِتْشِيل – بـشِيل – بِتْشِيلِي) الشنطـة الثَّقيلـة دِي كُلّ يـوم.

٦- إحْنـا دايمًا (بتسمَعُوا – بيسمعُوا – بِنِسْمَع) مُوسِيقَى هـادْيَة.

٧- إنتِي أحيانًا (بتِكْتِبي – بتِكْتِب – بِيكْتِب) جوابات لأصحـابِك.

٨- أنـا دايمًا (بيقْرا – بقْرا – بِتِقْرِي) قبل النـوم.

٩- همَّ (بيثْكَلَّمُوا – بِتثْكَلَّمُوا – بِنِثْكَلَّم) لُغات كتِيرة.

١٠- إنْتَ ليه (بِتِشْرَبِي – بِشْرَب – بِتِشْرَب) قَهْوَة كِتِير؟

Exercise 2
Complete each sentence by conjugating the habitual verb provided.

Example:

إحْنـا بِنْسـافِر لِبْنـان كُلّ صِيف. (بِيْسـافِر)

١- أنـا دايْمًا _____ قَرايْبِي يُوم الجُمْعَة. (بِيْزُور)

٢- هِيّ _____ شُقَق إيجار عَلَى طُول. (بِيلاقِي)

٣- إنْتُو _____ البِيتزا قَوِي. (بِيْحِبّ)

٤- الشَّغَّالَة _____ لَها الشَّقَّة مَرَّة كُلّ أُسْبُوع. (بِيْنَضَّف)

٥- إحْنـا _____ فِي كافِيتِيرْيا رِيش فِي وسْط البَلَد. (بيقعُد)

٦- إنْتَ _____ الأَسْتـاذ قُدَّام الفَصْل. (بِيسْتَنَّى)

٧- هُمَّ دايْمًا _____ كُورَة مَعَ أَصْحابْهُم. (بِيلْعَب)

٨- إنْتِي _____ معانِي الكَلِمـات الجَّدِيدَة بِسْهُولَة. (بِيفْهَم)

٩- هِيَّ _____ قَوِي فِي النَّادِي. (بِيِتْبِسِط)

١٠- أنا _____ بِسُرْعَة مِن شُغْل البِيت. (بِيِزْهَق)

Exercise 3
Talk about what you usually do in the following situations.

١- يوم عيد الربيع.

٢- أجازة الربيع

٣- قبل وبعد الفطار في رمضان (لمّا بتكونوا في بلد عربي).

٤- الكريسماس وراس السنة.

٥- عيد الحب.

٦- الهلاوين.

٧- عيد الشكر.

٨- أجازة الصيف.

٩- حفلة عيد ميلاد.

١٠- أيّ أعياد تانية.

Lesson 20: Negation of Habitual Verbs

There are two ways to negate habitual verbs.

Putting مِش *(miʃ)* Before the Verb

مِش بـسـافِر.	miʃ basaafir
I do not travel.	

Using the Prefix مَ *(ma)* and Suffix ش *(ʃ)*

↳ **Sound verbs**

To negate sound verbs—those without long vowels—leave the prefix بِـ *(bi)* with a *sukuun* (zero vowel), for all pronouns except أنـا *(ʔana)*, then add the prefix مَ *(ma)* and the suffix ش *(ʃ)* to the verb.

مَبْيِكْتِبْش	mabyiktibʃ
He does not write. / He is not writing (right now).	

Personal Pronoun	Negative Habitual Verb
هُوَّ huwwa he	مَبْيِكْتِبْش mabyiktibʃ
هِـيَّ heyya she	مَبْتِكْتِبْش mabtiktibʃ
هُمَّ humma they (d./p.)	مَبْيِكْتِبُوش mabyiktibuuʃ
إنْتَ ʔenta you (m. s.)	مَبْتِكْتِبْش mabtiktibʃ
إنْتِي ʔenti you (f. s.)	مَبْتِكْتِبِيش mabtiktibiiʃ

إنْتُو	مـبْتِكْتِبُوش
?entu	mabtiktibuuʃ
you (d./p.)	

أنـا	مـبـكْتِبْش
?ana	mabaktibʃ
I	

إحْنـا	مـبْنِكْتِبْش
?eħna	mabniktibʃ
we	

Hollow verbs (الفـعـل الأجـوف)

To negate hollow verbs—those with long vowels in the middle—shorten the long vowel then add the prefix مَ *(ma)* and the suffix ش *(ʃ)* to the verb.

مـبِيْرُحْش.	mabiyruħʃ
He does not go.	

Personal Pronoun	Negative Habitual Verb
هُوَّ	مـبِيْرُحْش
huwwa	mabiyruħʃ
he	
هِـيَّ	مـبِتْرُحْش
heyya	mabitruħʃ
she	
هُمَّ	مـبِيْرُحُوش
humma	mabiyruħuuʃ
they (d./p.)	
إنْتَ	مـبِتْرُحْش
?enta	mabitruħʃ
you (m. s.)	

إِنْتِي ʔenti you (f. s.)	مِبِتْرُحِيش mabitruḥiiʃ
إِنْتُو ʔentu you (d./p.)	مِبِتْرُحُوش mabitruḥuuʃ
أَنَا ʔana I	مَبرُحْش mabaruḥʃ
إِحْنَا ʔeḥna we	مِبِنْرُحْش mabinruḥʃ

Exercise 1
Choose the correct conjugation for each sentence.

Example:
هِيّ (بِيِدْرِس – بِتِدْرِسِي – بِتِدْرِس) فِي الْجَامْعَة الأَمْرِيكِيَّة.

١- إِنْتِي (مِبْخُدْش – مِبْتَخُدْش – مِبْتَخْدِيش) أَجَازْتِك السَّنَوِيَّة دِلوَقْتِي لِيه؟

٢- أَنَا (مِبْتِنْسَاش – مَبَنْسَاش – مِبْتِنْسِيش) واجِبَاتِي.

٣- هِيَّ (مِبِتْجِبِيش – مبِجِبْش – مِبِتْجِبْش) القَامُوس مَعاها الفَصْل.

٤- إِحْنَا (مِبْنِشْتِرِيش – مِبْتِشْتِرُوش – مِبِيشْتِرُوش) أَكْل مِن المَطْعَم دا.

٥- إِنْتَ (مِبْيِرْجَعْش – مِبْتِرْجَعْش – مِبْتِرْجَعِيش) مِن شُغْلَك بَدْرِي لِيه؟

٦- أَنَا (مبِشْرَبْش – مِبْتِشْرَبْش – مِبْيِشْرَبْش) شَاي تِقِيل.

٧ـ إِنْتُو لِيه (مِبِنْجِيش – مِبِيْجُوش – مِبِتْجُوش) عَند جِدُّكُو يُوم الْجُمْعَة؟

٨ـ أَنـا عـادَةً (مِبِيْرُحْش – مِبـرُحْش – مِبِتْرُحْش) الْجَـامْعَـة يُوم السَّبْت.

٩ـ إِنْـتِي دايْمَـا (مِبِتْسِبِيش – مِبِتْسِبْش – مِبِيْسِبْش) كُتُبِك فِي الْفَصْـل.

١٠ـ أَصْـحـابِـي (مِبْنِلْعَبْش – مِبْتِلْعَبُوش – مِبِيِلْعَبُوش) كُورَة فِي النَّـادِي دِلْوَقْتِي.

Exercise 2
Negate each of the following sentences.

Example:

أَنـا بِسـافِر كِتِـير.

أَنـا مِش بِسـافِر / مِبسـافِرْش كِتِـير.

١ـ هِيَّ بِتِصْحَى السَّاعَـة ٦ كُلَّ يُوم.

_____

٢ـ أَنـا بِتْـعَشَّى فِي مَطْعَم صِينِي دِلْوَقْتِي.

_____

٣ـ هُوَّ دايْمَـا بِيْشُوف أَصْـحـابُـه فِي الْجَّامْعَـة.

_____

٤ـ هُمَّ بِيِصْرِفُوا فُلُوسْـهُم مِن الْبَنْك دا.

_____

٥ـ هِيَّ بِتِتْكَلِّم ٣ لُغات.

_____

٦ـ إحْنـا دايْمًـا بِنِرْكَب أُتُوبِيس الجَّامْعَة.

٧ـ إنْتِي لِيه بِتِدِّي الشَّغَّالَة فُلُوس كِتِير؟

٨ـ همَّ دايْمًـا بِيِفْطَرُوا فـي النَّـادِي يُـوم الجُّمْعَة.

٩ـ إنْتُـو بِتِسْهَرُوا فِي قَهْوِة الفِيشـاوِي فِي رَمَضـان؟

١٠ـ إنْتَ دايْمًـا بِتْنـام بَدْرِي؟

Lesson 21: Future Tense Verbs, Affirmative and Negative

Sound Verbs

The future form (الـمـسـتـقـبـل) of sound verbs—those that do not have long vowels—is formed by adding the prefix حـ (ħa) to the unmarked present.

With the pronoun أنا (ʔana), drop the أ (ʔa) of the unmarked present and then add the future prefix.

حَيِشْرَب.	ħayiʃrab
He will drink.	

Personal Pronoun	Future Tense
هُوَّ huwwa he	حَيِشْرَب ħayiʃrab
هِيَّ heyya she	حَتِشْرَب ħatiʃrab
هُمَّ humma they (d./p.)	حَيِشْرَبُوا ħayiʃrabu
إنْتَ ʔenta you (m. s.)	حَتِشْرَب ħatiʃrab
إنْتِي ʔenti you (f. s.)	حَتِشْرَبِي ħatiʃrabi
إنْتُو ʔentu you (d./p.)	حَتِشْرَبُوا ħatiʃrabu

أَنـا	حَشْرَب
?ana	ħaʃrab
I	

إِحْنـا	حَنِشْرَب
?eħna	ħaniʃrab
We	

Weak Verbs

For weak verbs—hollow verbs and verbs ending with double consonants—keep the prefix of the unmarked present with its *sukuun* (zero vowel), for all pronouns except أَنـا (*?ana*), and add the prefix حَـ (*ħa*).

حَيْذاكِر.	ħayzaakir
He will study.	
حَيْحُطّ.	ħayhuʈʈ
He will put.	

Personal Pronoun	Future Tense	Future Tense
هُوَّ	حَيْذاكِر	حَيْحُطّ
huwwa	ħayzaakir	ħayhuʈʈ
He		
هِيَّ	حَتْذاكِر	حَتْحُطّ
heyya	ħatzaakir	ħathuʈʈ
She		
هُمَّ	حَيْذاكِرُوا	حَيْحُطُّوا
humma	ħayzakru	ħayhuʈʈu
they (d./p.)		

إِنْتَ ʔenta you (m. s.)	حَتْذاكِر ħatzaakir	حَتْحُطّ ħathuʃʃ
إِنْتِي ʔenti you (f. s.)	حَتْذاكْرِي ħatzakri	حَتْحُطّي ħathuʃʃi
إِنْتُو ʔentu you (d./p.)	حَتْذاكْرُوا ħatzakru	حَتْحُطُّوا ħathuʃʃu
أَنَا ʔana I	حَذاكِر ħazaakir	حَحُطّ ħahuʃʃ
إِحْنَا ʔeħna we	حَنْذاكِر ħanzaakir	حَنْحُطّ ħanhuʃʃ

Negation of Future

To negate future tense verbs, put the word مِش *(miʃ)* before the verb.

مِش حَسَافِر.	miʃ ħasaafir
I will not travel.	

Exercise 1
Choose the correct conjugation for each sentence..

Example:

هِيَّ (حرُوح – حَتْرُوح – حَتْرُوحِي) مَعَانَا.

١- هُمَّ (حتكونوا – حنكُون – حيكُونُوا) في البِيت بعد الضُّهْر.

٢- هِيَّ (حتِسْتَرَيَّح – حسْتَرَيَّح – حتِستَرَيَّحِي) شُوَيَّة عشـان تِعْبِت قـوِي فِـي الشُّغْل.

٣- هُوَّ مِش (حتِفْتِكِر – حيِفْتِكِر – حفْتِكِر) نمرِةْ تـليفون الشَّرْكَة.

٤- إِنْتِي (حرْكَب – حَتِرْكَب – حَتِرْكَبِي) القَطْر من إِسكِنْدِرِيَّة.

٥- أنـا (حشْتَغَل – حتِشْتَغَل – حتِشْتَغِلي) مـع خـالِي فِي مَصْنَعُـه الجَدِيد.

٦- إِحْنـا مِش (حتِتْفَرَّجُوا – حَنِتْفَرَّج – حَيِتْفَرَّجُوا) عَلى الفِيلْم فِي التَّلِيفِزْيُون معـاهُم.

٧- إِنْتَ (حتُقعُد – حيُقعُد – حقعُد) فِين فِي القـاهِرَة؟

٨- هِيّ مِش (حقْدَر – حتِقْدَرِي – حَتِقْدَر) تِعْمِل أكْل كِتير لِلْحَفْلَة.

٩- إِحْنـا مِش (حتْفَكَّرُوا – حَيْفَكَّرُوا – حَنْفَكَّر) فِي المُشْكِلَة دِي دِلْوَقْتِي.

١٠- إِنْتِي لِيه مِش (حسُوق – حَتْسُوقِي – حَتْسُوق) عربِيتِك بِنَفْسِك؟

Exercise 2

Retell the following story to explain what you would do next time to avoid having a bad experience.

أَحْجِز I reserve, book	نُجُوم stars	جُعْت I got hungry	طَرِيق road
عِطِشْت I got thirsty	عِطْلِت it broke down		مَعَدّتِش عَلَى I did not pass by
			دوّرت عَلَى I searched for
أغْطَس I dive	حَضَرْت I attended	تَجْرُبَة experience	سِيّئَة جِدًّا very bad

إمْبارِح بِاللّيـل قرَّرْت أرُوح شرم الشّيـخ. النّـهارْدَه الصُبْح صِحِيت بِدري قوي وفطِـرْت ولبِسـت هُدُومِـي ونِزِلْت من البِيت. مكـانْش عنـدِي وقْت أحْجِز تـذكِرة فـي الأتُـوبِيـس فَسُقْـت عربِيتِـي ولكـن طبـعًا مخَدتَّـهـاش لِلميكـانِيكِـي قَبْـل السَّفَـر. وعَشـان مِشِيـت مـن البِيت بِدرِي قوِي معَدِّتش عَلَـى السُّوبَر مارْكِت ومِشْتَرتْش أيّ حاجَـة. وفِـي الطَّريـق جُعْت وكمـان عطِشْت جدًّا لكن مكانْش معايـا أكُـل ولا مَيَّـة. عربِيتِـي عِطْلِـت فِـي الطَّريـق لكـن النّـاس ساعْدُونِـي ووصِلْـت شـرم. مكـانْش عَنْـدِي حجْـز فِـي أوتِيـل ٥ نُجُـوم فدوَّرت عَلَـى أوتِيـل عـادِي لكـن الخدمـة فِيـه مكـانِتْش كويسة قوي. شـرم كـانِت زحمـة قوي وعشـان كده مقدِرْتِش أغْطَـس زَيّ مـا كُنْت نـاوِي. بِاللّيـل حَضَـرْت حفلـة بسّ مشُفْتِش أيّ حدَ من أصحـابِـي عشـان مكـانُـوش يعْرَفُوا إنّـي فِـي شـرم. نِمْت فِـي الأوتِيـل وتـانِـي يـوم خـدتّ عربِيتِـي ورجِعْت البِيت. فِـي الحَقِيقَـة أنـا متْبَسطْـش خـالِص وقُلْـت إنّ دِي كـانِـت تـجْرُبَـة سيِّـئـة جدًّا.

Exercise 3
Use the future tense to talk about each of the following scenarios.

1. Your plans for the next weekend.
2. Your plans for a summer vacation.
3. Your plans for a visit to another country.
4. Your plans for getting a job or learning a foreign language.
5. Any other plans.

Lesson 22: Object Pronouns

Object pronouns (ضـمـائر الـمـفـعـول بـه) are pronominal suffixes attached to verbs (in all tenses) and function as direct or indirect objects of these verbs.

Subject Pronouns فـاعِل (Subject /Doer of the Action)	Object Pronouns مـفـعول بِـه (Direct / Indirect Object)
هُوَّ huwwa he	ـُه u him
هِـيَّ heyya she	ـهـا – هـا ha her
هُمَّ humma they (d. / p.)	ـهُم – هُم hum them (d. / p., m. / f.)
إنْـتَ ʔenta you (m. s.)	ـك ak you (m. s.)
إنْـتِـي ʔenti you (f. s.)	ـك ik you (f. s.)
إنْـتُـو ʔentu you (d. / p.)	كُـو – كُو ku you (d. / p., m. / f.)
أنـا ʔana I	نِـي – نِي ni me

إِحْنا	نـا – نَا
ʔeħna	na
we	us

The following are examples of how to use object pronouns with affirmative and negative verbs. With negative verbs, the object pronoun is attached to the verb before the ش *(ʃ)* suffix.

Object Pronoun	Affirmative Form	Negative Form
him	شافُه ← هُـ + هُوَّ شاف huwwa ʃaaf + u → ʃaafu he saw him	هُوَّ مشفُوش huwwa maʃafuuʃ he didn't see him
her	شافْها ← هـا + هُوَّ شاف huwwa ʃaaf + ha →ʃaafha he saw her	هُوَّ مشَفْهاش huwwa maʃafhaaʃ he didn't see her
them (d./p.)	شافْهُم ← هُم + هُوَّ شاف huwwa ʃaaf + hum → ʃaafhum he saw them	هُوَّ مشَفْهُمْش huwwa maʃafhumʃ he didn't see them
you (m. s.)	شافَك ← ـَك + هُوَّ شاف huwwa ʃaaf + ak → ʃaafak he saw you	هُوَّ مشَفَكْش huwwa maʃafakʃ he didn't see you
you (f. s.)	شافِك ← ـِك + هُوَّ شاف huwwa ʃaaf + ik → ʃaafik he saw you	هُوَّ مشَفْكِيش huwwa maʃafkiiʃ he didn't see you

you (d./p.)	هُوَّ شَاف + كُو ← شَافْكُو huwwa ʃaaf + ku → ʃaafku he saw you	هُوَّ مَشَفْكُوش huwwa maʃafkuuʃ he didn't see you
me	هُوَّ شَاف + نِي ← شَافْنِي huwwa ʃaaf + ni → ʃaafni he saw me	هُوَّ مَشَفْنِيش huwwa maʃafniiʃ he didn't see me
us	هُوَّ شَاف + نَا ← شَافْنَا huwwa ʃaaf + na → ʃaafna he saw us	هُوَّ مَشَفْنَاش huwwa maʃafnaaʃ he didn't see us

When verbs ending with long vowels ('aa,' 'uu,' 'ii'), in all tenses,
are attached to the object pronoun suffixes ـُه (him), ـَك (you, m. s.),
and ـِك (you, f. s.), a change in the pronunciation and the place of the
vowel preceding the object pronoun suffix takes place, as shown in
the following table.

Subject Pronoun	Object Pronoun	Affirmative Form	Negative Form
إِنْتِي ʔenti you (f. s.)	ـُه u him	إِنْتِي تِسْتَنِّي + ـُه ← تِسْتَنِّيه ʔenti tistanni + u → tistanniih you (f. s.) wait for him	إِنْتِي مَتِسْتَنِّيهُوش ʔenti matistannihuuʃ you (f. s.) do not wait for him
إِنْتُو ʔentu you (d./p.)	ـُه u him	إِنْتُو تِسْتَنُّوا + ـُه ← تِسْتَنُّوه ʔentu tistannu + u → tistannuuh you (d./p.) wait for him	إِنْتُو مَتِسْتَنُّهُوش ʔentu matistannuhuuʃ you (d./p.) do not wait for him

إِحْنَا	ـُه	إِحْنَا نِسْتَنَّى + ـُه ← نِسْتَنَّاه	إِحْنَا مِنِسْتَنَّهُوش
?eħna	u	?eħna nistanna + u → nistannaah	?eħna manistannahuuʃ
we	him	we wait for him	we do not wait for him
إِحْنَا	ـَك	إِحْنَا نِسْتَنَّى + ـَك ← نِسْتَنَّاك	إِحْنَا مِنِسْتَنَّكْش
?eħna	ak	?eħna nistanna + ak → nistannaak	?eħna manistannakʃ
we	you (m. s.)	we wait for you (m. s.)	we do not wait for you (m. s.)
إِحْنَا	ـِك	إِحْنَا نِسْتَنَّى + ـِك ← نِسْتَنَّاكِي	إِحْنَا مِنِسْتَنَّكِيش
?eħna	ik	?eħna nistanna + ik → nistannaaki	?eħna manistannakiiʃ
we	you (f. s.)	we wait for you (f. s.)	we do not wait for you (f. s.)

Exercise 1
Choose the correct verb + object for each sentence.

Example:

إِنْتَ (دَفَعْت + الـحِسـاب).
(دَفَعْتُـه – دَفَعْتَها – دَفَعْتِك)

١- هِيَّ (لِبْسِت + البِلُـوزَة).
(لِبْسِتِك – لِبْسِتْها – لِبْسِتُـه)

٢- أنـا (اِشْتَـرِيت + هِدِيَّة) لِمـامـا.
(اِشْتَرِيتْها – اِشْتَرِيتْهُم – اِشْتَرِيتُـه)

٣- إِحْنَا (اِسْتَنِّينـا + إِنْـتِي) قُدَّام الـجَّامْعَة.
(اِسْتَنِّينـاه – اِسْتَنِّينـاكِي – اِسْتَنِّنـاك)

٤- سَلْوى (كَلَّمِت + أنا) بِاللَّيل.
(كَلِّمِتَك – كَلِّمِتْها – كَلِّمِتْنِي)

٥- يُوسِف (قَرا + الْمَقالَة) مَرِّتِين.
(قَراها – قَراه – قَراك)

٦- هُو (شال + الفلُوس) فِي البَنك.
(شالُه – شالِك – شالْها)

٧- إنتُو (زُرْتُوا + لَيْلَى) الأسبُوع اللَّي فات.
(زُرْتُوها – زُرْتُوه – زُرْتُونِي)

٨- إحْنا (نِسِينا + الواجِب) فِي البِيت.
(نِسِيناها – نِسِيناه – نِسِيناك)

٩- هُمَّ (اتْعَشُّوا + سَمَك) فِي المَطْعَم الجِّدِيد.
(اتْعَشُّوها – اتْعَشُّوهُم – اتْعَشُّوه)

١٠- إنتَ (دَرَسْت + الْمُفْرَدات) كُوَيِّس.
(دَرَسْتُه – دَرَسْتَها – دَرَسْتِنِي)

Exercise 2
Complete each sentence by replacing the noun provided with the
correct pronominal suffix (object pronoun).

Example:

- أنا مِشْرِبْتِش + (الْعَصِير) ← **مِشْرِبْتُوش**

١- إنْتَ مِرُحْتِش + (الحَفْلَة)

_____

٢- أنا مِكَتَبْتِش + (الجَّواب)

_____

٣- إحْنا مِشُفْناش + (إنْتُو)

_____

٤ـ إنْتِي مِدَفَعْتِيش + (الـفـاتُـورَة)

_____

٥ـ إحْنـا مـلْعِبْنـاش + (تِنِس)

_____

٦ـ إنْتُـو مِتْكَلّمْتُوش + (فَرَنْسـاوِي)

_____

٧ـ لَيْلـى مزارِتْش + (أصْـحـابْـهـا)

_____

٨ـ هُمَّ مسابُوش + (الـشَّقَّة)

_____

٩ـ هِيَّ مطَبَخِتْش + (الأكْل)

_____

١٠ـ إنْتُـو مِدَرَسْتُوش + (الـعَرَبِـي)

_____

Exercise 3
In the following passage, replace the nouns in parenthesis with the correct pronominal suffixes (object pronouns).

إمْبـارِح يُوسِف كـان عنده مشكلـة في شُغْلُـه. الـصُّبـح كلّمت (يُوسِف) _____
وبـعديـن قابِلْـت (يُوسِـف) _____ وخَـدتّ (يُوسِـف) _____ ورُحْنـا
الـكـافيتيريـا. هنـاك شُفْنـا ليلـى ويُوسِف كلّم (ليلـى) _____ وإدّى (ليلى)
_____ جـواب للـمديـر. ليلـى خـدت (الـجَّـواب) _____ وإنّت (الـجَّـواب)
_____ للـمديـر. المديـر قـرا (الـجَّواب) _____ وشَكَـر (ليلـى)
_____ وإدّى (يُوسِـف) _____ أجـازة.

Exercise 4
Rewrite the passage in exercise 3, negating each verb (with its object pronoun).

Lesson 23: The Imperative (Commands)

There are two types of the imperative form (فـعـل الأمـر) in Arabic: direct commands (أمـر مـبـاشـر) and indirect commands (أمـر غـيـر مـبـاشـر).

Direct Commands

To form direct affirmative commands, return the verb to its unmarked present tense form (without the habitual ـبِ *(bi)* or the future ـحَ *(ħa)* prefix), then drop the prefix ـيَ *(y)* used with the unmarked present for the pronoun هـو *(huwwa)* and add the appropriate suffixes as shown in the following tables.

Verbs of two consonants

Past Tense	Unmarked Present	Imperative (you, m. s.)	Imperative (you, f. s.)	Imperative (you, d./p.)
كَل	يـاكُل	كُل	كُلِي	كُلُوا
kal	yaakul	kul	kuli	kulu
to eat				
خَد	يـاخُد	خُد	خُدِي	خُدُوا
xad	yaaxud	xud	xudi	xudu
to take				

Exception: the verb جَـه *(gah)*

Although جَـه (transliteration: *gah*; meaning: to come) is a verb of two consonants, its command is formed from a different verb: تَـعـالـى *(taʒala)*.

Past Tense	Unmarked Present	Imperative (you, m. s.)	Imperative (you, f. s.)	Imperative (you, d./p.)
جَـه	يِـجِـي	تَـعـالـى	تَـعـالِي	تَـعـالـوا
gah	yigi	taʒala	taʒali	taʒalu
to come				

Verbs of two consonants with the second consonant doubled

Past Tense	Unmarked Present	Imperative (you, m. s.)	Imperative (you, f. s.)	Imperative (you, d./p.)
بَصّ	يِبُصّ	بُصّ	بُصّي	بُصُّوا
baṣṣ	yibuṣṣ	buṣṣ	buṣṣi	buṣṣu
to look				

Verbs of three consonants

Replace the unmarked present tense prefix ـِ *(y)* with the prefix إ *(i)* then add the appropriate suffixes as shown in the table below.

Past Tense	Unmarked Present	Imperative (you, m. s.)	Imperative (you, f. s.)	Imperative (you, d./p.)
عَمَل	يِعْمِل	اِعْمِل	اِعْمِلي	اِعْمِلوا
ʒamal	yiʒmil	iʒmil	iʒmili	iʒmilu
to do / make				

Hollow verbs

Past Tense	Unmarked Present	Imperative (you, m. s.)	Imperative (you, f. s.)	Imperative (you, d./p.)
شَاف	يِشُوف	شُوف	شُوفي	شُوفُوا
ʃaaf	yiʃuuf	ʃuuf	ʃuufi	ʃuufu
to see				

Exception

In Egyptian Colloquial Arabic, sometimes the command is not formed from the same unmarked present verb but from a different verb (as was the case with the verb جـه).

Past Tense	Unmarked Present	Imperative (you, m. s.)	Imperative (you, f. s.)	Imperative (you, d./p.)
جـاب gaab to bring	يِجِيب yigiib	هـات haat	هـاتِي haati	هـاثُوا haatu

Verbs of four letters

Past Tense	Unmarked Present	Imperative (you, m. s.)	Imperative (you, f. s.)	Imperative (you, d./p.)
قـابِل ʔaabil to meet	بِقـابِل yiʔaabil	قـابِل ʔaabil	قـابْلِي ʔabli	قـابْلُوا ʔablu

Verbs of more than four letters
Replace the unmarked present tense prefix ـِ (y) with the prefix إ (i) then add the appropriate suffixes as shown in the table below.

Past Tense	Unmarked Present	Imperative (you, m. s.)	Imperative (you, f. s.)	Imperative (you, d./p.)
إتْفَرَّج ʔitfarrag to watch	يِتْفَرَّج yitfarrag	إتْفَرَّج itfarrag	إتْفَرَّجِي itfarragi	إتْفَرَّجُوا itfarragu

Verbs ending in long vowels
For verbs that end with ى (alif maksuura, 'broken a') or ي (long 'ii') in the unmarked present, add the prefix إ (i) and the appropriate suffixes and also drop the ى or ي for the pronouns إنْتِي (ʔenti) and إنْتُو (ʔentu).

Past Tense	Unmarked Present	Imperative (you, m. s.)	Imperative (you, f. s.)	Imperative (you, d./p.)
اِسْتَنَّى istanna to wait for	يِسْتَنَّى yistanna	اِسْتَنَّى istanna	اِسْتَنِّي istanni	اِسْتَنُّوا istannu
اِشْتَرَى iʃtara to bring	يِشْتِرِي yiʃtiri	اِشْتِرِي iʃtiri	اِشْتِرِي iʃtiri	اِشْتِرُوا iʃtiru

☾ **Negating direct commands**

To negate direct commands, use the negative form of the unmarked present.

Negative Imperative (you, m. s.)	Negative Imperative (you, f. s.)	Negative Imperative (you, d./p.)
مَتِشْرَبْش matiʃrabʃ Don't drink!	مَتِشْرَبِيش matiʃrabiiʃ Don't drink!	مَتِشْرَبُوش matiʃrabuuʃ Don't drink!

Indirect Commands

☾ **Suggestions**

　　 مَا (ma) + **affirmative unmarked present**

This structure can be translated as "Why don't you . . . ?"

مَاتْسَافِر إِسْكِنْدِرِيَّة؟	matsaafir-iskindiriyya (m. s.)
مَاتْسَافْرِي إِسْكِنْدِرِيَّة؟	matsafri-skindiriyya (f. s.)
مَاتْسَافْرُوا إِسْكِنْدِرِيَّة؟	matsafru-skindiriyya (d./p.)
Why don't you travel to Alexandria?	

　　 بَلاش (balaaʃ) + **affirmative unmarked present**

This structure can be translated as "There is no need to . . . ."

بَلاش تـاكُل بَرَّه.	balaaʃ taakul barra (m. s.)
بَلاش تـاكْلِي بَرَّه.	balaaʃ takli barra (f. s.)
بَلاش تـاكُلُوا بَرَّه.	balaaʃ taklu barra (d./p.)
There is no need to eat out / Don't eat out.	

Warnings

إوْعَى (ʔiwʒa) and إيَّاك (ʔiyyaak) are used either to warn somebody not to do something or to urge somebody to do something. Their meaning depends on the context and on who is addressing who: whether it is a parent to a child, a boss to an employee, a friend to a friend, and so on.

إوْعَى (ʔiwʒa) / إوْعِي (ʔiwʒi) / إوْعُوا (ʔiwʒu) + affirmative unmarked present

With an affirmative verb, this structure warns someone away from doing something and urges them not to do it.

إوْعَى تُخْرُج. أنا قُلْت لَك.	ʔiwʒa tuxrug ʔana ʔultilak (m. s.)
إوْعِي تُخْرُجِي. أنا قُلْت لِك.	ʔiwʒi tuxrugi ʔana ʔultilik (f. s.)
إوْعُوا تُخْرُجُوا. أنا قُلْت لكُو.	ʔiwʒu tuxrugu ʔana ʔultilku (d./p.)
Don't go out, I told you (warning).	
إوْعَى تِسْهَر عَشان إنْتَ عَيَّان.	ʔiwʒa tishar ʒaʃan-inta ʒayyaan (m. s.)
إوْعِي تِسْهَرِي عَشان إنْتِي عَيَّانَة.	ʔiwʒi tishari ʒaʃan-inti ʒayyaana (f. s.)
إوْعُوا تِسْهَرُوا عَشان إنْتُو عَيَّانِين.	ʔiwʒu tisharu ʒaʃan-intu ʒayyaaniin (d./p.)
I urge you not to stay up late because you're sick.	

إوْعَى (ʔiwʒa) / إوْعِي (ʔiwʒi) / إوْعُوا (ʔiwʒu) + negative unmarked present

With a negative verb, this structure urges someone to do something and warns them against not doing it.

إِوْعَى مَتِشْتِرِيش الـهَدِيَّة.	ʔiwʒa matiʃtiriiʃ-ilhidiyya (m. s.)
إِوْعِي مَتِشْتِرِيش الـهَدِيَّة.	ʔiwʒi matiʃtiriiʃ-ilhidiyya (f. s.)
إِوْعُوا مَتِشْتِرُوش الـهَدِيَّة.	ʔiwʒu matiʃtiruuʃ-ilhidiyya (d./p.)
You have to buy the gift.	

إِيَّاك (*ʔiyyaak*) / إِيَّاكِي (*ʔiyyaaki*) / إِيَّاكُوا (*ʔiyyaaku*) +
affirmative unmarked present
With an affirmative verb, this structure warns someone from doing
something and urges them not to do it.

إِيَّاك تِمْشِي قَبْل مَا تْخَلَّص واجْبَك.	ʔiyyaak timʃi ʔabl-i-ma-txallaş wagbak (m. s.)
إِيَّاكِي تِمْشِي قَبْل مَا تْخَلَّصِي واجْبِك.	ʔiyyaaki timʃi ʔabl-i-ma-txallaşi wagbik (f. s.)
إِيَّاكُوا تِمْشُوا قَبْل مَا تْخَلَّصُوا واجْبْكُو.	ʔiyyaaku timʃu ʔabl-i-ma-txallaşu wagibku (d./p.)
Don't leave before finishing your homework.	

إِيَّاك (*ʔiyyaak*) / إِيَّاكِي (*ʔiyyaaki*) / إِيَّاكُوا (*ʔiyyaaku*) + **negative**
unmarked present
With a negative verb, this structure urges someone to do something,
and warns against not doing it.

إِيَّاك مَتَعْمِلْش الـوَاجِب.	ʔiyyaak mataʒmilʃ-ilwaagib (m. s.)
إِيَّاكِي مَتِعْمِلِيش الـوَاجِب.	ʔiyyaaki matiʒmiliiʃ-ilwaagib (f. s.)
إِيَّاكُوا مَتِعْمِلُوش الـوَاجِب.	ʔiyyaaku matiʒmiluuʃ-ilwaagib (d./p.)
You have to do your homework.	
إِيَّاك مَتْجِيش الْحَفْلَة.	ʔiyyaak matgiiʃ-ilħafla (m. s.)
إِيَّاكِي مَتْجِيش الْحَفْلَة.	ʔiyyaaki matgiiʃ-ilħafla (f. s.)
إِيَّاكُوا مَتْجُوش الْحَفْلَة.	ʔiyyaaku matguuʃ-ilħafla (d./p.)
Don't think about not coming to the party / You have to come to the party.	

Exercise 1
Choose the correct command for each sentence.

Example:

يـا بَنـات (اِعْمِـل ـ اِعْمِلِـي ـ <u>اِعْمِلُوا</u>) الـواجِب.

١- يـا هُدَى (إوْعَـى ـ إوْعِـي ـ إوْعُـوا) تِشِيلِـي كُتُب تِقِيلَـة.

٢- يـا أوْلاد (كُل ـ كُلِـي ـ كُلُوا) السَّنْدُوِتْشـات كُلَّهـا.

٣- يـا أسـاتْذَة (رُوح ـ رُوجِي ـ رُوحُوا) الاجتِمـاع عَلَـى طُـول.

٤- يـا عَلِي (اِصْحَـى ـ اِصْحِي ـ اِصْحُوا) بَدْرِي.

٥- يـا بَنـات (متْبِعْش ـ متْبِعِيش ـ متْبِيعُوش) البِيت بِالتَّمَن دَا.

٦- يـا يُوسِف (إوْعَـى ـ إوْعِـي ـ إوْعُـوا) تِنْسَـى الْـواجِب.

٧- يـا نَـدَى (اِشْرَب ـ اِشْرَبِـي ـ اِشْرَبُـوا) قَهْوِتِك.

٨- يـا طُلَّاب (إيّـاك ـ إيّـاكِي ـ إيّـاكُو) متْذاكْرُوش لِلامْتِحـان.

٩- يـا لَيْلَـى (اِتْغَدَّى ـ اِتْغَدِّي ـ اِتْغَدُّوا) مَعـانـا.

١٠- يـا سَلْـوَى (متْسِبْش ـ متْسِبِيش ـ متْسِيبُوش) شُغْلِك الجِّدِيد.

Exercise 2
Give directions in the form of direct commands—once to a man, then to a woman, and then to more than one person—to go to each of these places: a university, a railway station, a computer center, a supermarket, and a bank.

الصّينية / المِيدان	عَلى طُول	شِمال	يِمين
square	straight on	left	right
فَوق	تَحْت	قَبْل	بَعْد
above / on top of	below / under	before	after
هِناك	هِنا	النَّفَق	الكوبْري
there	here	tunnel	bridge

Exercise 3

In the following recipe, change the underlined commands from (إنْتَ) to (إنْتِي) and (إنْتُو). Read the recipe to your class.

طريقة عمل المكرونة بصلصة الطماطم
المقـادير
نصّ كيلو مكرونة
معلقتين كُبار سمنة
بصلـة كبيرة مبشورة
كوبَّايْتِين عصير طماطم
ملح
أُسْلُـق المكرونـة فـي حَلَّـة وضِيـف لـها مَعْلَقَـة كبيـرة ملـح لِحَدّ مـا تِسْتِـوِي وبَعْدِيـن صَفّـي المكرونـة وأُشْطُفْهـا. بعـد كِـده إقْـدَح السَّمنـة وحَمَّـر فيهـا البصلـة لغايـةْ مـا تِصْفَرّ. ضِيـف عصيـر الطماطـم وسِيبُـه لحدّ مـا المَيَّـة تِجِـفْ وتِظْهـر السمنـة. اخْلِـط المكرونـة بالصلصـة وقَدَمْهـا سُخْنـة.

Exercise 4

Create a recipe for each of the following, using commands addressed to (إنْتَ), (إنْتِي), and (إنْتُو). Read it to your class.

أومليـت
بطـاطس محمَّـر
شـاي بِلَبـن
سَلَطـة
عَصير لَمُون

Exercise 5
Rewrite each sentence using the imperative form of the verb.

Example:

إحْنـا نـاوْيـيـن نِـرُوح السِّيـنِـمـا.
رُوحُوا السِّيـنِـمـا.

١- هـي عـايـزة تـسـافـر بـكـرة.

_____

٢- إحـنـا لازم نـذاكـر كـويـس.

_____

٣- هـو نـاوي يـشـتـري عـربـيـة.

_____

٤- إحـنـا مـسـتـحيـل نـنـسـى شـنـطـنـا فـي الـفـصـل.

_____

٥- هـي عـايـزة تـحطّ فـلـوسـهـا فـي الـبـنـك.

_____

٦- هـو رايـح يـحـجـز فـي الـقـطـر.

_____

٧- إحـنـا مـش عـايـزيـن نـشـوف فـيـلـم الـرعـب دا.

_____

٨- هـي مـش نـاويـة تـسـيـب الـبـيـت.

_____

٩- هو ضروري يستريِّح من تعب الشغل.

_____

١٠- إحنا مهم نقدِّم طريقة عمل الأومليت.

_____

Exercise 6
Negate each of the following sentences.

Example:

اِشْترُوا هُدُوم جِدِيدَة.

مَتِشْتِرُوش هُدُوم جِدِيدَة.

١- العبوا رياضة كتير.

_____

٢- حطِّي شنطتك على المكتب.

_____

٣- هات شاي من الكافيتيريا.

_____

٤- اتفرَّجوا على فيلم في السِّينما.

_____

٥- سافِر الصبح.

_____

٦- اتعلَّمي المفردات الجديدة من القاموس.

_____

٧- اتغدَّى مع أصحابَك.

_____

٨ـ ارجعي البيت متأخَّر.

_____

٩ـ اشتروا الطلبات من السوبر ماركت دا.

_____

١٠ـ استلف منها ٢٠٠ جنيه.

_____

Lesson 24: Conditional Sentences

The conditional sentence (الـجـمـلـة الـشـرطـيـة) consists of three parts: a conditional particle (أداة شـرط) + a conditional clause (جـمـلـة الـشـرط) + a result clause (جـواب الـشـرط).

There are two types of conditional sentences:

1. Real conditional: a conditional which could possibly come true.

2. Unreal conditional: a conditional which cannot come true, either due to the passage of time or because it contradicts reality.

Real Conditional Sentences

After the conditional particles إذا (?iza) and إنْ (?in), the verb in the conditional clause must be in the past tense, even if the understood English meaning uses the present tense. After the conditional particle لـو (law), the verb in the conditional clause can be in the past (as with the other conditional particles), but it can also be in any other tense.

The following table shows examples of real conditional sentences after the conditional particles إنْ, إذا, and لـو.

Conditional Particle	Tense in Conditional Clause	Tense in Result Clause	Example
إذا / إنْ / لـو ?iza / ?in / law if	past (+ -)	future (+ -)	إذا/إن/لـو ذاكِرْت حَتِفْهَم ?iza/?in/law zakirt ḥatifham If you study [Arabic: "studied"], you will understand
إذا / إنْ / لـو ?iza / ?in / law if	past (+ -)	imperative (+ -)	إذا/إن/لـو تِعِبْت مـتُـخْـرُجْـش ?iza/?in/law tiʒibt matuxrugʃ If you get [Arabic: "got"] tired, do not go out

إذا / إنْ / لَو	past (+ -)	modal + unmarked present (+/-)	إذا/إنْ/لَو سـافِرْت لازِم تِقـابْلُـه
?iza / ?in / law if			?iza/?in/law saafirt laazim ti?ablu If you travel [Arabic: "traveled"], you must meet him
إذا / إنْ / لَو	past (+ -)	present habitual (+/-)	إذا/إنْ/لَو زِهِقْت بـارُوح الـنَّـادِي.
?iza / ?in / law if			?iza/?in/law zihi?t baruuḥ-innaadi If I get [Arabic: "got"] bored, I go to the club

The following table shows examples of real conditional sentences with the particle لَو and the conditional clause in other tenses.

Conditional Particle	Tense in Conditional Clause	Tense in Result Clause	Example
لَو law if	future (+/-)	future (+/-)	لَوْ مِش حَتِقْدَر تـاخُد أجـازَة مِش حَتِقْدَر تسـافِر مَعـانـا. law miʃ ḥati?dɑr taaxud ?agaaza miʃ ḥati?dɑr tisaafir maʒaana If you can't take a vacation, you won't be able to travel with us

لَو	future (+/-)	imperative (+/-)	لَوْ حَتِرْجَعِي بَذْرِي كَلِّمِينِي
law			law ḥatirgaʒi badri kallimiini
if			If you're going to return early, call me
لَو	future (+/-)	modal + unmarked present (+/-)	لَوْ حَتِيجِي مُمْكِن أَقَابِلْهَا
law			law ḥatiigi mumkin ʔaʔabilha
if			If she's coming, it will be possible for me to meet her
لَو	modal + unmarked present (+/-)	modal + unmarked present (+/-)	لَوْ لَازِم تِمْشِي ضَرُورِي تِقُول لُه
law			law laazim timʃi ḍaruuri tiʔullu
if			If you have to leave, you should tell him
لَو	modal + unmarked present (+/-)	imperative (+/-)	لَوْ لَازِم تُزُورُوه خُدُونِي مَعَاكُو
law			law laazim tuzuruuh xuduuni maʒaaku
if			If you (d./p.) have to visit him, take me with you

لَو	modal + unmarked present (+/-)	future (+/-)	لَوْ لازِم تِخَلَّص البَحْث حاساعْدَك
law			law laazim tixallaṣ-ilbaħs ħasaʒdak
if			If you have to finish the research, I will help you

Note: (+/-) indicates affirmative/negative

Unreal Conditional Sentences

As previously stated, an unreal conditional is one that cannot come true, either due to the passage of time or because it contradicts reality. The conditional particle لَو *(law)* must be used in unreal conditionals. The following table shows some examples of unreal conditionals.

Conditional Particle	Tense in Conditional Clause	Tense in Result Clause	Example
لَو	past (+/-)	كان + past (+/-)	لَوْ كُنْت الْوَزِير كُنْت ساعِدتّ كُلّ النَّاس
law			law kunt-ilwaziir kunt saʒitt-i-kull-innaas
if			If I were the minister, I would have helped all the people
لَو	كان + past (+/-)	كان + future (+/-)	لَوْ كان جَه إمْبارِح كان حَيْشُوفْهُم
law			law kaan gah-imbaariħ kaan hayʃufhum
if			If he had come yesterday, he would have seen them

لَو	+ كـان	+ كـان	لَوْ كـان راح هِنـاك كـان شـافْنـي.
law	past (+/-)	past (+/-)	law kaan raaħ hinaak kaan ʃafni
if			If he had gone there, he would have seen me

Note: (+/-) indicates affirmative/negative

Exercise 1
Match each conditional clause in the right-hand column with the appropriate result clause in the left-hand column.

لازِم يِدُّوا لُـه فُلُـوسُه	١- لَو كـانِت قَدِّمِت لِلـوَظيفَـة
مِش حَنِـقْدَر نِدْفَعْـهـا تـانِـي	٢- إذا جِيـت
لازِم تِـجيبْـهـا جِديـدَة	٣- إن اتْغدّينـا يُـوم الـخَـميـس بَرّه
كـانِت خَدِتْـهـا	٤- لَو مِش حَنِدْفَع الـفـاتُورَة بُكْرَة
اتْكَلِّمُوا مَعاه	٥- إن اشْتَـريت عَرَبِيَّة
مِش حـاقُـول لُكُـو حـاجَـة	٦- لَو خَلَّـصْـتِـي شُغْـلِك
لازِم تِـذاكِـر كُوَيِّس	٧- إن قـابِلْـتُـوا الـمُـديـر
بِنِتْغَدَّى يُـوم الـجُـمْـعَـة فِـي الـبِـيت	٨- لَو بـاعُـوا الـبِـيت
حَتْشُـوف كُـل أصْحـابَـك	٩- إذا كـان عَنْدِك امْتِـحـان
رُوحِـي الـحَفْـلَـة	١٠- لَو قـابِلْـتُـكُو

Exercise 2
Mark each sentence as correct or incorrect, and rewrite those that are incorrect.

Example:
إذا حـارُوح الـحـفـلـة لازِم أشُوفْـهُـم. (X)
إذا رُحْت الـحـفـلـة لازِم أشُوفْـهُـم.

١- لَو كـانُـوا جُـم كـانُـوا قـابْلُـونـا.

٢- إنْ كـانِت طِفْلَة كُنْت اشْتَرِيت لَها لِعْبَة.

_____

٣- لـو كـان أخُوهـا كـان عِرِفْهـا.

_____

٤- إذا كُنَّـا سـافِرْنـا معـاهُم كُنَّـا اتْبَسَطْنـا.

_____

٥- إنْ مِتْعَشِّتْش حـاكُل معـاكُو.

_____

٦- إذا حَتْخَلَّصُوا شُغْلُكُو بِسُرْعَة ارْجَعُوا عَلَى طُول.

_____

٧- إذا كُنْتِي عـايْزَة لَبَن اتَّصْلِي بالسُّوبَر مـارْكِت.

_____

٨- إذا بـازْهَق بـارُوح النَّـادِي.

_____

٩- إنْ كان عَنْدِي قَصْر كُنْت عَزَمْت كُلّ أصْحـابِي.

_____

١٠- إذا شَرَحْتِي لُه الْمُشْكِلَة مُمْكِن يِسـاعْدِك.

_____

Exercise 3
Translate each sentence into Arabic.

1. If she reads the newspaper, she will know the problem.

_____

2. If we arrive early, we should visit our neighbor.

_____

3. If you (f. s.) get fed up, talk to your friends.

_____

4. If I were a famous singer, people would love me.

_____

5. If we have to eat something, we will eat fish.

_____

6. If she had listened to him, he would have been happy.

_____

7. If you (m. s.) have to buy a new shirt, tell me.

_____

8. If we have to travel tomorrow, we have to finish our work today.

_____

9. If I am not going to Alexandria, I might visit Luxor.

_____

10. If I had been there, I would have watched the new film.

_____

Exercise 4
Complete each conditional sentence.

١ ـ لَو كُنت طِفِل/ـة _____

٢ ـ لَو كُنت مِلْيُونِير _____

٣ ـ لَو كُنت الْمُطْرِبَة أُمّ كَلثُوم _____

٤ ـ لَو كُنت الرَّئِيس _____

٥ ـ لَو كُنت زُوِيل _____

٦ ـ لَو كُنت رَئِيس الوُزراء _____

٧ ـ لَو كُنت الأَدِيب نَجِيب مَحْفُوظ _____

٨ ـ لَو كُنت أَشْهَر صَحَفِي _____

٩ ـ لَو كُنت مَلِكِةُ جَمـال مَصْر _____

١٠ ـ لَو كُنت أَشْهَر لاعِب كُرِةُ قَدَم _____

Lesson 25: The Active Participle

The active participle (اسم الـفـاعـل) is a noun derived from a verb. It performs a variety of functions, such as describing stable states or recent past actions whose effect is still felt in the present.

Formation of the Active Participle
ᕲ Verbs of two consonants

To form the active participle from verbs that consist of two consonants, insert the prefix وا *(waa)*. For the masculine form, put a *kasra* (short 'i') below the second to last letter. For the feminine and dual/plural forms, add the appropriate endings too.

Past Tense	Active Participles		
	Masculine Singular	Feminine Singular	Dual / Plural (m. / f.)
خَـد xad to take	واخِـد waaxid	واخْـدة waxda	واخْـدِيـن waxdiin

ᕲ Verbs of two consonants, with the second doubled

To form the active participle for verbs with two consonants in which the second consonant is doubled, insert ١ *(ʔalif)* after the first letter of the root. In the masculine form, break the doubling and put a *kasra* (short 'i') below the second to last letter. In the feminine and dual/ plural forms, keep the doubling and also add the appropriate endings.

Past Tense	Active Participles		
	Masculine Singular	Feminine Singular	Dual / Plural (m. / f.)
بَصّ baṣṣ to look	بـاصِـص baaṣiṣ	بـاصّـة baṣṣa	بـاصّـيـن baṣṣiin

ᕲ Sound verbs of three consonants

To form the active participle of sound verbs—those that do not have long vowels—insert ١ *(ʔalif)* after the first consonant of the root. For the masculine form, put a *kasra* (short 'i') below the second to last letter (the second consonant of the root). For the feminine and dual/ plural forms, put a *sukuun* (zero vowel) on this letter, then add the appropriate endings.

Past Tense	Active Participles		
	Masculine Singular	Feminine Singular	Dual / Plural (m. / f.)
عَمَل	عامِل	عامْلة	عامْلِين
ʒamal	ʒaamil	ʒamla	ʒamliin
to do / make			

❧ **Verbs ending with ا (ʔalif) or ى (ʔalif maksuura)**
To form the active participle of weak verbs of three consonants that end with ا *(ʔalif)* or ى *(ʔalif maksuura*, 'broken a'*)*, insert an ا after the first letter of the root. For the masculine singular form, change the final ا or ى to a ي (long 'ii'). For the feminine singular and the dual/plural forms, change the final ا or ى to a ـﻴ *(y)* then add the appropriate endings.

The following table shows examples of the masculine, feminine, and dual/plural active participles.

Past Tense	Active Participles		
	Masculine Singular	Feminine Singular	Dual / Plural (m. / f.)
قرا	قاري	قارية	قاريـين
ʔara	ʔaari	ʔarya	ʔaryiin
to read			
رمـى	رامـي	رامية	رامـيـين
rama	raami	ramya	ramyiin
to throw			

◟ Verbs ending with ي (long 'ii')

To form the active participle of weak verbs of three consonants that end with ي (long 'ii'), insert an ا *(ʔalif)* after the first letter of the root. For the masculine form, keep the ي at the end. For the feminine singular and the dual/plural forms, change the ي to a ـي *(y)* then add the appropriate endings as shown in the following table.

Past Tense	Active Participles		
	Masculine Singular	**Feminine Singular**	**Dual / Plural (m. / f.)**
مِشْي	مـاشِـي	مـاشْـيَـة	مـاشْـيِـين
miʃi	maaʃi	maʃya	maʃyiin
to walk / leave			

◟ Hollow verbs of three consonants

To form the active participle, insert a ـي *(y)* after the middle ا *(ʔalif)* then follow the patterns shown in the following table.

Past Tense	Active Participles		
	Masculine Singular	**Feminine Singular**	**Dual / Plural (m. / f.)**
شـاف	شـايِـف	شـايْـفَـة	شـايْـفِـين
ʃaaf	ʃaayif	ʃayfa	ʃayfiin
to see			

◟ Verbs with more than three letters

To form the active participle, add the prefix ـم *(mi)* to the root. For the masculine form, put a *kasra* (short 'i') below the second to last letter. For the feminine and dual/plural forms, also add the appropriate ending.

	Active Participles		
Past Tense	Masculine Singular	Feminine Singular	Dual / Plural (m. / f.)
قابِل ʔaabil to meet	مِقابِل miʔaabil	مِقابْلَة miʔabla	مِقابْلِين miʔabliin
اِسْتَعْمِل ʔistaʒmil to use	مِسْتَعْمِل mistaʒmil	مِسْتَعْمِلَة mistaʒmila	مِسْتَعْمِلِين mistaʒmiliin

Functions of the Active Participle

Describing stable states

The active participle describes a stable, ongoing state in which a person is not performing any action; that is, there is no physical movement or change in the situation.

هُوَّ نـايِم دِلْوَقْتِي.	huwwa naayim dilwaʔti
He's asleep now.	
هِيَّ قـاعْدَة عَلـى الكُرسِي.	heyya ʔaʒda ʒa-kkursi
She's sitting on the chair.	
هو لابِس قمـيص.	huwwa laabis ʔamiiş
He's wearing a shirt.	

This is in contrast to the habitual tense where the action happens often, as something habitual, or the action is still in process.

هو عـادةً بيلـبس قمـيص أبـيض.	huwwa ʒadatan biyilbis ʔamiiş ʔabyaḍ
He usually wears a white shirt.	
هو دلـوقتـي بيلـبس.	huwwa dilwaʔti biyilbis
He's putting on his clothes right now.	

هِيَّ بِتُقعُد عَلى الكُرسِي دِلوَقْتِي.	heyya bituʒʒud ʒa-kkursi dilwaʔti

She's sitting on the chair now.

The following are some of the most commonly used active participles that indicate an ongoing state.

English Translation	Masculine Singular	Feminine Singular	Dual / Plural (m. / f.)
asleep / sleeping	نـايم naayim	نـايمـة nayma	نـايمـين naymiinn
awake	صـاحـي şaaħi	صـاحـيـة şaħya	صـاحـيـين şaħyiin
smelling	شـامِـم ʃaamim	شـامَّـة ʃamma	شـامِّـيـن ʃammiin
riding	راكِب raakib	راكْبَـة rakba	راكْبِـين rakbiin
sitting / staying	قـاعد ʔaaʒid	قـاعدة ʔaʒda	قـاعدين ʔaʒdiin
standing	واقف waaʔif	واقفـة waʔfa	واقـفيـن waʔfiin
seeing	شـايـف ʃaayif	شـايفـة ʃayfa	شـايفيـن ʃayfiin
hearing	سـامِع saamiʒ	سـامِعـة samʒa	سـامِعـيـن samʒiin
feeling	حـاسِـس ħaasis	حـاسَّـة ħassa	حـاسِّـيـن ħassiin
walking / leaving	مـاشِـي maaʃi	مـاشْـيَـة maʃya	مـاشِـيـيـن maʃyiin

waiting for	مـسـتـنّـي mistanni	مـسـتـنّـيـة mistanniyya	مـسـتـنّـيـيـن mistanniyyiin
living	عـايـش ʒaayiʃ	عـايْـشَـة ʒayʃa	عـايْـشـيـن ʒayʃiin
knowing	عـارِف ʒaarif	عـارْفَـة ʒarfa	عـارْفِـيـن ʒarfiin
remembering	فـاكِـر fakir	فـاكْـرَة fakra	فـاكْـريـن fakriin
forgetting	نـاسِـي naasi	نـاسْـيَـة nasya	نـاسْـيِـيـن nasyiin
understanding	فـاهِـم faahim	فـاهْـمَـة fahma	فـاهْـمِـيـن fahmiin

↳ **Describing the recent past**

The active participle can express a recent past action whose effect is still felt in the present time.

A:	مـا تـاكُل مَـعـانـا؟	mataakul maʒaana
	Why don't you eat with us?	
B:	شـكـرًا أنـا واكِـل.	ʃukran ʔana waakil
	Thanks, I've already eaten / I'm full.	

This is in contrast to the simple past where the action is complete.

أنـا كلـت فـي الـجـامـعـة إمـبـارح.	ʔana kalt f-iggamʒa-mbaarih
I ate at the university yesterday.	

The following example contrasts the active participle and the simple past.

بـلاش تـجيب فـاكـهـة الـنّـهـارده مـانـتَ مشـتـري إمبـارح	
balaaʃ tigiib fakha-nnahaarda manta miʃtiri-mbaariħ	
Don't buy fruit today, you bought some yesterday.	
أنـا اشـتـريـت مـوز إمبـارح	ʔana-ʃtareet mooz-imbaariħ
I bought bananas yesterday.	

The following are some of the most commonly used active participles that indicate the recent past.

English Translation	Masculine Singular	Feminine Singular	Dual / Plural (m. / f.)
to drink	شـارب ʃaarib	شـاربـة ʃarba	شـاربـيـن ʃarbiin
to eat	واكـل wakil	واكـلـة wakla	واكـلـيـن wakliin
to have breakfast	فـاطـر faaṭir	فـاطـرة faṭra	فـاطـريـن faṭriin
to have lunch	مـتـغدّي mitɣaddi	مـتـغدّيـة mitɣaddiyya	مـتـغدّيـيـن mitɣaddiyyiin
to have dinner	مـتـعشّي mitʒaʃʃi	مـتـعشّـيـة mitʒaʃʃiyya	مـتـعشّـيـيـن mitʒaʃʃiyyiin
to buy	مِشـتِري miʃtiri	مِشـتِريّـة miʃtiriyya	مِشـتِريّـيـن miʃtiriyyiin
to sell	بـايِـع baayiʒ	بـايْـعَـة bayʒa	بـايْـعِيـن bayʒiin
to bring	جـايِـب gaayib	جـايْـبَـة gayba	جـايْـبِيـن gaybiin

⌣ Describing the near future

A number of active participles which imply movement can be used to indicate the near definite future. The active participles in this category are sometimes used interchangeably with the future tense.

A	هو الْمُدِير موجود؟	huwwa-ilmudiir mawguud
	Is the manager there / here / present?	
B	لأ دا خرج وراجِع / وحَيِرْجَع بَعْد رُبْع ساعَة.	
	laʔ da xarag wi-raagiʒ / wi-ḥayirgaʒ baʒd-i-rubʒ-i-saaʒa	
	No, he's gone out and will be back in fifteen minutes.	

The following are some of the most commonly used active participles indicating the near future.

English Translation	Masculine Singular	Feminine Singular	Dual / Plural (m. / f.)
going	رايح / raayiḥ	رايحة / rayḥa	رايحين / rayḥiin
coming	جايّ / gayy	جايّة / gayya	جايّين / gayyiin
traveling	مسافر / misaafir	مسافرة / misafra	مسافرين / misafriin
returning	راجِع / raagiʒ	راجعة / ragʒa	راجعين / ragʒiin
going out	خارج / xaarig	خارجة / xarga	خارجين / xargiin
entering	داخِل / daaxil	داخلة / daxla	داخلين / daxliin
getting down	نازِل / naazil	نازلة / nazla	نازلين / nazliin

going up	طالِع	طالِعة	طالِعين
	ʃaaliʒ	ʃalʒa	ʃalʒiin

↳ Describing attitudes, emotions, and physical conditions

The active participle also expresses attitudes, emotions, and physical conditions. For this usage, it is formed using a different pattern: add the suffix ان (aan) to the past tense of the pronoun هو (huwwa).

English Translation	Past Tense	Masculine Singular	Feminine Singular	Dual / Plural (m. / f.)
tired	تِعب	تَعْبان	تَعْبانة	تَعْبانين
	tiʒib	taʒbaan	taʒbaana	taʒbaniin

The following are some of the most commonly used active participles indicating attitudes, emotions, and physical conditions.

English Translation	Masculine Singular	Feminine Singular	Dual / Plural (m. / f.)
tired	تَعْبان	تَعْبانة	تَعْبانين
	taʒbaan	taʒbaana	taʒbaniin
sick	عَيَّان	عَيَّانة	عَيَّانين
	ʒayyaan	ʒayyaana	ʒayyaniin
happy	فرْحان	فرْحانة	فرْحانين
	farħaan	farħaana	farħaniin
upset	زَعْلان	زَعْلانة	زَعْلانين
	zaʒlaan	zaʒlaana	zaʒlaniin
worried	قَلْقان	قَلْقانة	قَلْقانين
	ʔalʔaan	ʔalʔaana	ʔalʔaniin
fed up / bored	زَهقان	زَهْقانة	زَهقانين
	zahʔaan	zahʔaana	zahʔaniin

cold	بَرْدان	بَرْدانَة	بَرْدانِين
	bardaan	bardaana	bardaniin
hot	حَرّان	حَرّانَة	حَرّانِين
	ħarraan	ħarraana	ħarraniin
warm	دَفْيان	دَفْيانَة	دَفْيانِين
	dafyaan	dafyaana	dafyaniin
hungry	جَعـان	جَعـانَة	جَعـانِـين
	gaʒaan	gaʒaana	gaʒaniin
full (opposite of hungry)	شَبْعـان	شَبْعـانَة	شَبْعـانِين
	ʃabʒaan	ʃabʒaana	ʃabʒaniin
thirsty	عَطْشـان	عَطْشـانَة	عَطْشـانِين
	ʒaṭʃaan	ʒaṭʃaana	ʒaṭʃaniin

➤ Describing the state of the subject or direct object

The active participle can occur after the verb in a verbal sentence, where it acts as حـال (ħaal), describing the state of the subject or the direct object.

بيروح الجـامـعة مـاشي.	biyruuħ-iggamʒa maaʃi
He goes to the university on foot. (The active participle describes the subject.)	
شفتها قـاعدة في الكـافيتيـريـا.	ʃuftaha ʔaʒda fi-kkafitirya
I saw her sitting in the cafeteria. (The active participle describes the direct object.)	

➤ Describing occupations and professions

The active participle can also refer to occupations.

نـجـيب محـفـوظ كـاتـب مصـري.	Nagiib Maħfuuz̧ kaatib maṣri
Naguib Mahfouz is an Egyptian writer.	

هـي دي مُدرّسِةُ الـفـصـل.	heyya di mudarrisit-ilfaşl
This is the class teacher.	

Describing the recent past or an unchanged state (using لِسَّه)
When the active participle is preceded by the word لِسَّه *(lissa)*,
depending on the context, it can either mean "just" to refer to the
recent past or "still" to refer to a state that has not changed.

	عـلـي خرج الـصـبـح ولِسَّه راجِع دلـوقـتـي.	ʒali xɑrɑg-işşubħ wi-lissa raagiʒ dilwaʔti
This is the class teacher.	Ali left in the morning and he just came back.	
A	مـنـى صـحـيـت؟	muna şiħyit
	Did Mona wake up?	
B	لأ لِسَّه نـايـمـة.	laʔ lissa nayma
	No, she's still asleep.	

Exercise 1
Complete each sentence by selecting the correct form of the active
participle.

Example:

ـ الـبِـنْـت _____ الـعَـرَبِـيَّة إمْـبـارِح.
(شـارِي – <u>شـارْيَـة</u> – شـارْبِـين)

١ـ إنْـتَ _____ مِن إسْـكِـنـدِرِيَّـة بُـكْرَة؟
(جـايّ – جـايّـة – جـايِّـين)

٢ـ إنْـتُـو مِش _____ الـحَـفْـلَـة.
(رايِـح – رايْـحَـة – رايْـحِـين)

٣ـ هُـمَّ لِسَّـة _____ الـمُـدير الـجِّـديـد.
(مِـقـابِـل – مِـقـابْـلَـة – مِـقـابْـلِـين)

٤ـ إحـنـا _____ كُوَيِّس لـلامْتِحـان.
(مِذاكِر – مِذاكْرَة – مِذاكْرين)

٥ـ هِيَّ _____ فُسْتـان جَمِيـل.
(لابِس – لابْسَة – لابْسِين)

٦ـ إنْتِـي _____ أجـازَة الأسْبُـوع الـجَّايّ.
(واخِد – واخْدَة – واخْدِين)

٧ـ هُـوَّ _____ بَعْد شُوَيَّة.
(خـارِج – خـارْجَـة – خـارْجِين)

٨ـ هِيَّ لِسَّة _____ شُغْلَها.
(سايِب – سايْبَة – سايْبِين)

٩ـ إحْنـا _____ كِتِير مِن شُوَيَّة.
(واكِل – واكْلَـة – واكْلِين)

١٠ـ هُمَّ _____ فِي الـكَّافِيتِيرْيـا دِلْوَقْتِـي.
(قاعِد – قاعْدَة – قاعْدِين)

Exercise 2
Change the verb in each sentence from the past tense to the active participle.

Example:

إنْتَ صِحِيت بَدْري. إنْتَ صاحِي بَدْري.

١ـ إحْنـا مِشِينـا السَّاعَـة ٣.

_____

٢ـ هِيَّ اتْعَشِّت سَمَك وسَلَطَـة.

_____

٣ـ إنْتُـو اشْتَرِيتُـوا فاكْهَـة.

_____

٤- هُوَّ نـام مِتْأَخَّر.

٥- هُمَّ سـافِرُوا بـالْـقَطِر.

٦- إنْتِي جِبْتِي هِدِيَّة لِمـامْتِك.

٧- إنْتَ صَرَفْت ١٠٠ جِنِيه.

٨- هِيَّ راحِت الجَّامْعـة.

٩- إنْتُو غَسَلْتُوا هُدُومْكُو.

١٠- إنْتِي اتْعَلِّمْتِي إيطـالِي.

Exercise 3
Translate each sentence, choosing whether to use an active
participle, the past tense, the habitual form of a verb, the present
continuous, or the future tense.

Example:
They (have) just had lunch.

هُم لِسَّة مِتْغَدِّيِّين.

---

1. He is asleep now.

---

2. We are traveling to Europe after two years.

---

3. She met her relatives last year.

_____

4. You (f. s.) always drive your car on the holidays.

_____

5. My friends are walking into the garden now.

_____

6. We are going to the party at night.

_____

7. You (p.) are coming back from Lebanon this week.

_____

8. They studied for tomorrow's exam.

_____

9. We've just watched this movie.

_____

10. He is waiting for the bus in front of the university.

_____

Appendix: Verbs in the Past Tense and the Unmarked Present

English Translation	Past	Unmarked Present
to be	كَان kaan	يِكُون yikuun
to be able to	قِدِر ʔidir	يِقْدَر yiʔdɑr
to become	بَقَّى baʔa	يِبْقَّى yibʔa
to bring / buy	جَاب gaab	يِجِيب Yigiib
to buy	اِشْتَرَى ʔiʃtara	يِشْتِرِي yiʃtiri
to carry	شَال ʃaal	يِشِيل yiʃiil
to clean	نَضَّف naḍḍɑf	يِنَضَّف yinaḍḍɑf
to close	قَفَل ʔafal	يِقْفِل yiʔfil
to come	جَه gah	يِجِي yiigi
to come back / return	رِجِع rigiʒ	يِرْجَع yirgaʒ

to do / make	عَمَل	يِعْمِل
	ʒamal	yiʒmil
to drink	شِرِب	يِشْرَب
	ʃirib	yiʃrab
to drive	ساق	يِسُوق
	saaʔ	yisuuʔ
to eat	كَل	ياكُل
	kal	yaakul
to enter	دَخَل	يُدْخُل
	daxal	yudxul
to feel	حَسّ بِـ	يِحِسّ بِـ
	ħass bi	yiħiss bi
to find	لَقَى	يِلاقِي
	laʔa	yilaaʔi
to finish	خَلَّص	يِخَلَّص
	xallaṣ	yixallaṣ
to forget	نِسِي	يِنْسَى
	nisi	yinsa
to get down / descend	نِزِل	يِنْزِل
	nizil	yinzil
to get fed up / bored	زِهِق	يِزْهَق
	zihiʔ	yizhaʔ
to get tired	تِعِب	يِتْعَب
	tiʒib	yitʒab
to give	اِدَّى	يِدِّي
	ʔidda	yiddi
to go	راح	يِرُوح
	raaħ	yiruuħ

to go out / exit	خَرَج	يُخْرُج
	xarag	yuxrug
to go up	طِلِع	يِطْلَع
	ʃiliʒ	yiʃlaʒ
to have a nice time	إِنْبَسَط / إِتْبَسَط	يِنْبِسِط / يِتْبِسِط
	ʔinbasaʃ / ʔitbasaʃ	yinbisiʃ / yitbisiʃ
to have breakfast	فِطِر	يِفْطَر
	fiʃir	yifʃar
to have dinner (a light, late meal)	إِتْعَشَّى	يِتْعَشَّى
	ʔitʒaʃʃa	yitʒaʃʃa
to have lunch (a main meal)	إِتْغَدَّى	يِتْغَدَّى
	ʔitɣadda	yitɣadda
to happen	حَصَل	يِحْصَل
	ħaṣal	yiħṣal
to hear	سِمِع	يِسْمَع
	simiʒ	yismaʒ
to know	عِرِف	يِعْرَف
	ʒirif	yiʒraf
to learn	إِتْعَلَّم	يِتْعَلَّم
	ʔitʒallim	yitʒallim
to study	دَرَس	يِدْرِس
	daras	yidris
to leave behind / quit	سَاب	يِسِيب
	saab	yisiib
to like / love	حَبّ	يِحِبّ
	ħabb	yiħibb

to look	بَصّ	يِبُصّ
	baṣṣ	yibuṣṣ
to lose	خِسِر	يِخْسَر
	xisir	yixsar
to meet	قابِل	يِقابِل
	ʔaabil	yiʔaabil
to open	فَتَح	يِفْتَح
	fataḥ	yiftaḥ
to pay	دَفَع	يِدْفَع
	dafaʒ	yidfaʒ
to play	لِعِب	يِلْعَب
	liʒib	yilʒab
to put	حَطّ	يِحُطّ
	ḥaṭṭ	yiḥuṭṭ
to read	قَرا	يِقْرا
	ʔara	yiʔra
to remember / think (guess)	اِفْتَكَر	يِفْتِكِر
	ʔiftakar	yiftikir
to rest	اِسْتَرَيَّح	يِسْتَرَيَّح
	ʔistarayyaḥ	yistarayyaḥ
to ride	رِكِب	يِرْكَب
	rikib	yirkab
to run	جِري	يِجْري
	giri	yigri
to say	قال	يِقُول
	ʔaal	yiʔuul

to see	شـاف ʃaaf	يِشُـوف yiʃuuf
to sell	بـاع baaʒ	يبيـع yibiiʒ
to sit / stay	قَعَد ʔaʒad	يُقعُد yuʒʒud
to sleep / go to sleep	نـام naam	يِنـام yinaam
to smell (transitive)	شَمَّ ʃamm	يِشِـمَّ yiʃimm
to speak (to)	كَلِّم / اِتْكَلِّم مَعَ kallim / itkallim maʒa	يِكَلِّم / يِتْكَلِّم مَعَ yikallim / yitkallim maʒa
to spend (money)	صَرَف ṣaraf	يِصْرِف yiṣrif
to stand / stop	وِقِف wiʔif	يُقَف yuʔaf
to stay up late	سِـهِر sihir	يِسْهَر yishar
to study (on one's own)	ذاكِر zaakir	يِذاكِر yizaakir
to take	خَد xad	يـاخُد yaaxud
to take off (clothes)	قَلَع ʔalaʒ	يِقْلَع yiʔlaʒ
to think / remind	فَكَّر fakkar	يِفَكَّر yifakkar

to travel	سـافِر	يِسافِر
	saafir	yisaafir
to turn down (volume)	وَطَّى	يِوَطِّي
	waṭṭa	yiwaṭṭi
to turn up (volume)	عَلَّى	يِعَلِّي
	ʒalla	yiʒalli
to understand	فِهِم	يِفْهَم
	fihim	yifham
to use	اِسْتَعْمِل	يِسْتَعْمِل
	istaʒmil	yistaʒmil
to visit	زار	يِزُور
	zaar	yizuur
to wait for	اِسْتَنَّى	يِسْتَنَّى
	istanna	yistanna
to wake up / get up	صِحِي	يِصْحَى
	ṣiħi	yiṣħa
to wake up / get up / stand up	قام	يِقُوم
	ʔaam	yiʔuum
to walk / leave	مِشِي	يِمشِي
	miʃi	yimʃi
to wash	غَسَل	يِغْسِل
	ɣasal	yiɣsil
to watch	اِتفَرَّج عَلَى	يِتفَرَّج عَلَى
	itfarrag ʒala	yitfarrag ʒala
to wear / get dressed	لِبِس	يِلْبِس
	libis	yilbis

to win	كِسِب	يِكْسَب
	kisib	yiksab
to work	اِشْتَغَل	يِشْتَغَل
	iʃtaɣal	yiʃtaɣal
to write	كَتَب	يِكْتِب
	katab	yiktib